PERSO
FINANCIAL
PLANNING

Andrew Burgess and Chris Jones

60p

PUBLISHED IN ASSOCIATION WITH
NEVILLE RUSSELL
CHARTERED ACCOUNTANTS

Kogan
Page

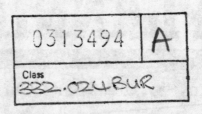
First published in Great Britain by
Kogan Page Ltd, 120 Pentonville Road,
London N1 9JN

British Library Cataloguing in Publication Data

Burgess, Andrew
  Personal financial planning.
  1. Finance, Personal – Great Britain
  I. Title   II. Jones, Chris
  332.024'00941   HG179

  ISBN 1-85091-206-8 5x

Printed and bound in Great Britain by
Biddles Ltd, Guildford

Contents

Appendices   137

Index   147

Introduction

Personal financial planning is a much used phrase with a wide variety of meanings. It may simply mean switching assets from one place to another to increase the income being earned. It may mean restructuring business arrangements to gain maximum tax benefits. It may mean involving a more complicated trust arrangement to obtain the most flexible and tax efficient structure.

Personal financial planning means assessing your present situation, finding out where you want to be and then planning the best route to get there. Each individual has different needs.

This book is intended to help you to find your way through the financial planning maze. In the first part you will find set out some of the basic ground rules of planning to help mitigate the impact of income tax, capital gains tax and inheritance tax. The second part looks at some specific areas of planning in particular situations such as within the family. We have tried in the third part to shed some light on the wide range of investments available today. Here you will find some background notes on how the investments work and in each case a table which summarises the tax treatment, the advantages and disadvantages of each type of investment, together with an indication of the particular circumstances in which the investment can be most beneficial.

This book contains the appropriate provisions of the Finance Act 1986. Inevitably, it provides general information. You may need specific advice and, to help you, a simple questionnaire has been inserted after the index. If you would like to complete this and send it to Andrew Burgess of Neville Russell, he can contact you by telephone or arrange a meeting to discuss the situation in more detail.

PART 1
THE GROUND RULES

Chapter 1

Income Tax

Introduction

The UK tax system operates on a cumulative basis during each tax year which runs from 6 April. All the income which is assessable for that year (not necessarily the same as the income earned in the year because some income, eg trading profits, is taxed in the year after that in which it is earned) is aggregated. From the total are deducted the various reliefs and allowances to which you are entitled. The remaining income is taxed in bands at increasingly higher rates up to a maximum of 60% which for 1986/87 applies to taxable income over £41,200. (Details of the rates are in Appendix 5.) What this means is that if you have taxable income of at least £41,200 in 1986/87, you will pay tax of at least £16,823 and, for every further pound you earn, you will pay 60p of it in income tax.

Residence status

All income which arises in the UK is taxable here irrespective of where the recipient lives. If you are resident in the UK for tax purposes and you are also domiciled in the UK, you are taxable on your worldwide income. Your residence and domicile status are questions of fact which will be determined by the Inland Revenue and if you are considering making a change in your status you should seek advice as to the steps you should take. High income earners often consider going into tax-exile but there are many pitfalls to catch the unwary.

If you are resident but not domiciled you will be taxed on all your UK income and any income arising elsewhere in the world to the extent that you bring it into the UK, or are effectively able to enjoy it in the UK (this does not apply if you are a citizen of Eire). Before you come to the UK you should try to ensure that your funds are segregated into separate capital and income accounts and that wherever possible you only transfer to the UK funds from your capital account. See Part 2.

Allowances

Our tax system gives individuals, with the exception of married

11

women, a personal allowance. These allowances have to be notified as soon as possible. If you have not made a claim for a particular year you may do so at any time up to six years later. The allowances which are currently available are:

- *single person:* this is the basic allowance;
- *wife's earned income:* available where a wife is working. You can only claim the full allowance if the wife's earnings at least equal that amount;
- *married man's allowance:* this is also known as the higher personal allowance and is available where man and wife are living together and in certain circumstances where they are separated. The allowance is reduced for the year of marriage depending on when in the year the marriage took place, but there is no reduction in the year in which a wife dies. The allowance is not available to a couple living together as 'man and wife' but not married. It is, however, available to a working wife whose husband is not working;
- *additional personal allowance:* available to those not entitled to a higher personal allowance but who have children living with them. A married man can claim this if his wife is totally incapacitated;
- *widow's bereavement allowance:* a widow is entitled in the year of bereavement and the following year of assessment (provided she has not remarried before the start of it) to an allowance equivalent to the additional personal allowance;
- *age relief:* an individual who becomes 65 in a year of assessment and whose income is below a specified limit (£9,400 for 1986/87) is entitled to claim age relief for that year and subsequent years. In the case of a married couple the allowance can be claimed from the time the elder spouse reaches 65 years of age. The age relief is higher than either of the basic personal allowances but once the income limit is reached the excess is reduced by £2 for every £3 of income over the limit;
- *dependent relative:* this is given to individuals who maintain at their own expense any incapacitated relative or mother or mother-in-law who is widowed or divorced or separated. The allowance is higher where the claimant is a single woman;
- *housekeeper:* a small allowance is available in certain limited circumstances;
- *blind person:* an allowance is due where either the individual or his wife is a registered blind person. The allowance is doubled where both husband and wife are blind;

- *daughter's or son's services:* old or infirm people who are dependent on the services of a son or daughter who lives with them and is maintained by them can claim this small allowance.

Loss reliefs

Where you sustain a loss in a business which you can show is being run on commercial lines you can claim relief in respect of that loss. The loss will normally be carried forward and set against profits from the same business in subsequent years but you can claim to set it against:

- other income of the year in which the loss was made. This goes first against your other earned income, then against any investment income and then against any income of your wife;
- other income of the year after that in which the loss was sustained to the extent that the loss has not been used against current income;
- if the business is still in its first four years of operation you can set the loss back against other income received three years earlier and subsequent years until all the loss has been used. So a loss sustained in 1986/87 could be set against other income for 1983/84, then 1984/85 and then 1985/86.

All claims for loss relief must be made within two years of the end of the year of assessment in which the loss was incurred and a checklist of time limits for 5 April 1987 is in Appendix 4.

Deferral and advancement of income

Income tax planning should never be regarded as an exercise to be carried out for one year in isolation: you should look at a 2-3 year period at least, and longer if possible. Within this period you should see if it is possible so to arrange your pattern of income that income can be moved from years of relatively high taxation to years when you know your tax bill will be lower. This does, of course, depend upon how much control you may have over the flow of your income.

Deferral of income can be particularly worthwhile if you are close to the income limit for age allowance.

The deferral of income may not affect the amount of tax you pay but it could substantially affect the date on which you pay the tax. For example, if as controlling shareholder/director of a company you decide to vote a dividend of £50,000, the higher rate tax due on that amount must be paid by 1 December following the end of the year of assessment in which the payment is made. If the dividend is paid on 31 March 1987, tax will be due on 1 December 1987; if payment is delayed until 7 April 1987, tax will not have to be paid until 1 December 1988.

Chapter 2

Capital Gains Tax

Introduction
Capital gains tax (CGT) was introduced in 1965 and taxes gains made on the disposal of certain types of assets. The term *disposal* is widely drawn and covers not only sales but also gifts, transfers at under-value and some types of compensation for the loss of an asset. In its simplest form CGT taxes the difference between the disposal proceeds and original cost but, as will become apparent, the simple case very rarely arises. There are however many ways of mitigating or deferring CGT.

Residence status
You may be caught for CGT if you are resident or ordinarily resident in the UK when you make the disposal. *Ordinarily resident* means habitually resident so that, even if you are not physically in the UK for the year in which you make a disposal, you may still be chargeable to CGT if you cannot satisfy the Revenue that you became not ordinarily resident.

Domicile status
If you are UK domiciled, you are chargeable in respect of the disposal of assets held anywhere in the world. If you are not domiciled here you will only be charged to CGT on overseas assets to the extent that you remit proceeds to the UK. Again therefore care must be taken in organising remittances so that capital remitted comes first from non-taxable sources.

Timing disposals
CGT is payable by 1 December following the year of assessment in which the disposal took place. Where you are planning to dispose of an asset you should try to plan the disposal for early in the tax year rather than towards the end of it to allow the maximum enjoyment of the full proceeds.

Annual exemption
If the total of net gains does not exceed £6,300 in 1986/87, you are

not liable to CGT. The excess over this figure is taxable at 30%. Husband and wife share a single exemption. If you have large capital gains, it is advisable to make full use of this exemption each year, perhaps by 'bed and breakfasting' if necessary.

Indexation

In 1982 the Government introduced indexation to try to remove the inflationary element from chargeable gains. Substantial improvements were made to the allowance by the Finance Act 1985 for disposals after 6 April 1985 and the main elements are now as follows:

- indexation applies from the date on which the asset was acquired or March 1982 if later;
- the indexation allowance is computed by reference to the retail price index and is applied to the cost of the asset and any allowable improvements;
- a loss can be increased by indexation and a gain can be turned into a loss;
- for an asset held on 31 March 1982 a claim can be made to compute indexation by reference to the market value of the asset at that date rather than by reference to original cost.

The changes made in 1985 have altered the rules for identifying shares. It is particularly worth noting that 'bed and breakfasting' which had become less attractive is now advantageous again.

Assets acquired pre 1965

CGT applies on the element of any gain accruing from 6 April 1965. Where assets acquired before that date are sold the gain is usually apportioned on a time basis but it is possible to elect for the gain to be calculated by reference to the market value of the asset on 6 April 1965. Such a claim must be made within two years of the end of the year of assessment in which the disposal was made.

Losses

Allowable losses are taken into account in determining net gains for the year. Where total gains do not exceed the annual exemption any realised losses may be wasted. Losses not used in any year are carried forward but are only used in subsequent years to the extent to which they reduce net gains to the annual exemption level. Care should therefore be exercised to ensure that maximum advantage is taken by making efficient use of losses, perhaps by postponing their realisation or by balancing them with gains. The particular situation of disposals by married couples is dealt with in Part 2.

Reliefs for gifts

Where a gift is made from one individual to another who is resident in the UK, an election may be made to hold over any gain deemed to have been made by the donor. The recipient is generally treated as having acquired the asset at the base cost to the donor. Where there is a sale at an under value and the consideration exceeds the donor's allowable cost, that excess cannot be held over and a chargeable gain will arise.

This relief is important since careful planning may result in substantial tax savings. For example, a transfer at an under value before 5 April may be considered to use the donor's (and, perhaps, the recipient's) annual CGT exemption.

Where a gift on which this relief is claimed is made after 5 April 1981, if the donee emigrates within 6 years, other than temporarily, the gain held over will become chargeable. This might be avoided if the donee settles the assets before emigrating.

Relief for gifts into settlement

The general relief for gifts between individuals applies also to gifts into a settlement. The trust must be resident and ordinarily resident in the UK (and not dual resident) and a charge to tax on the gain held over will arise if, at any time, it ceases to be resident whilst holding the assets.

Consideration could be given to settling cash in the trust and then arranging for the trustees to buy the assets at an appropriate price which enables the settlor to obtain the maximum benefit from losses and annual exemptions.

Relief for transfer by trustees

The relief can also be claimed where assets are resettled or distributed by the trustees to beneficiaries, provided that the beneficiary is resident in the UK and does not emigrate within 6 years.

Subject to Inheritance Tax considerations, use of this provision could be very advantageous where the beneficiaries are not already using their annual CGT exemption since assets with a capital gain could be realised by the beneficiaries rather than the trustees.

Roll-over relief

A person who disposes of a business asset and reinvests the proceeds (not just the amount of the gain) in new business assets may defer the charge to CGT. There is no requirement for the old and new assets to be used in the same trade. The new asset must be acquired within

17

a four year period beginning a year before the date of disposal of the old asset.

Retirement relief

A businessman may obtain relief from CGT once he reaches the age of 60 or has to retire on grounds of ill health. The relief, which can be up to £100,000, is given against gains arising from the disposal of business interests. This can include shares in a family trading group. The scope of the relief has been considerably widened by Finance Act 1985.

Chapter 3
Inheritance Tax

Introduction

Inheritance Tax (IHT) was introduced in the Finance Act 1986 to replace Capital Transfer Tax (CTT). The change took place with effect from 18 March 1986. In many respects IHT closely resembles the old Estate Duty which was replaced by CTT in 1974.

Where an individual makes a gift to another individual or into an accumulation and maintenance trust or into a trust for the disabled, no IHT will be payable at the time the transfer is made. This gift will be known as a potentially exempt transfer. If it subsequently transpires that the gift was made within seven years of the donor's death it will be charged to IHT at the appropriate death rate. That charge will be reduced by a prescribed percentage if the gift had been made more than three years before death. Details of the tax rates are given in Appendix 5.

Other gifts made by an individual during his lifetime, typically gifts into trusts, will be chargeable to IHT at half the death rate applicable at the time of the gift. This charge could be increased if the transfer takes place within seven years of death because the rates applicable at the date of death (subject to any tapering) will be applied. Where this calculation would result in a lower tax charge there is no provision for repayment.

The rates of IHT which are chargeable on death are essentially the same as those for CTT and the impact of the tax on an estate will be every bit as devastating. The need for careful and early planning remains paramount.

Value of transfer

The value of each chargeable transfer is measured by the difference in the value of the transferor's estate before and after the transfer. There can be a substantial difference between the value lost and the value gained. For example, a disposal of 2% of shares in a company could take the transfer from a 51% to a 49% holding causing a large reduction in the value of the estate but the increase in the recipient's estate would be small. Considerable care needs to be taken in planning such transactions.

Residence and domicile

Residence has no bearing on IHT liabilities, domicile is the key factor. If you are domiciled in the UK, all your worldwide assets are in the scope of IHT but if you are non-domiciled, only assets situated in the UK are liable. This gives rise to planning possibilities. For example, the UK home of a non domiciled individual may be held in an overseas company so that it remains property outside the UK for tax purposes.

Exemptions

Substantial IHT savings can be made by making systematic use of available exemptions:

- *Gifts between spouses*: these are exempt without limit (whether made during lifetime or on death) unless the transferor spouse is UK domiciled and the transferee spouse is not. In this case only the first £55,000 is exempt.
- *£250 small gifts exemption*: this exemption applies to small outright gifts made in the tax year but there is no limit to the number of recipients. This exemption cannot be claimed where more than £250 is given to any person in a tax year.

  Example: On 10 October, A gives £250 to each of his 13 grandchildren. Each gift is exempt, falling within this exemption (he had made no previous gifts). The next day, he decides to give a further £500 to B (one of the grandchildren). This increases the total gift to B to £750 and means that the £250 exemption cannot be claimed in respect of the gift to B.

- *£3,000 annual exemption*: this applies to the total gifts made by a transferor in each tax year. If it has not been fully used, the balance of the previous year's exemption may be brought forward for one year only and used when that of the current year has been fully utilised.
- *Normal expenditure exemption*: covers transfers of net income after tax provided that they form part of normal (ie typical or habitual) expenditure and leave sufficient income for the transferor to maintain his usual standard of living. It is necessary to submit a claim for this exemption.
- *Gifts in consideration of marriage*: these are exempt up to a limit of £5,000 from each parent, £2,500 from each grandparent and £1,000 from any other person. Either party to the marriage may give the other £2,500.
- *Provision for dependants*: certain gifts for the support and

maintenance of children and dependent relatives are not charged to IHT.
- *Charities*: gifts to charity are exempt without any limit.

Potentially exempt transfers will not be regarded as using up the exemptions at the time they are made.

You must make sure that you use all your exemptions as fully as possible each year.

Nil rate band
A substantial part of all chargeable (ie non exempt) transfers, whether during lifetime or on death, are taxed at a nil rate. The nil rate band for 1986/87 is £71,000 and this is index-linked so that a small increase can be expected each year. The nil rate threshold provides important tax planning opportunities particularly when used in conjunction with the inter-spouse exemption and other reliefs such as those for business and agricultural property. Significantly, husband and wife each have their own nil rate band.

Cumulation
When CTT was first introduced, all chargeable transfers made by an individual were cumulated to establish the rate of CTT applicable to each successive gift. Since 6 April 1981 however chargeable transfers have been cumulated only with those made within the previous 10 years. This period has now been reduced to seven years. Where chargeable transfers are to be made these should take place at the earliest possible opportunity.

Trusts
Under CTT it was possible to gift assets into a trust, effectively retain control of them by acting as a trustee and potentially be able to benefit from any growth in value which would take place outside your own estate. The IHT provisions on gifts with reservation mean that where you are a beneficiary under a new settlement (pre 18 March 1986 settlements are not affected) the assets comprised in the settlement will remain part of your estate until you release your interest. Provided you exclude yourself from benefit (although it may be possible for your spouse to be a beneficiary) a trust will continue to be an effective IHT planning tool. See Part 2.

Interest free loans
It is possible to make interest free loans without any IHT liability arising, provided that the loan does not reduce your estate ie it must

be repayable on demand. The Finance Act 1986 does however contain anti-avoidance provisions dealing with certain other loans. There are some potential income tax problems and care must be taken with these also.

Reliefs

Reductions of up to 50% in the value of gifts can be obtained where those gifts are of assets which qualify for either business property relief or agricultural property relief. Assets include business assets, holdings of unquoted shares and agricultural land. In each case the asset must have been owned for at least two years. Additionally, new rules have been introduced for IHT requiring the donee to continue to own the assets as business property.

PART 2
PLANNING

Chapter 4

Planning within the Family

Financial planning within the family context breaks down into six separate areas:

- Protecting the family
- Minimising income tax
- Minimising capital gains tax
- Mitigating inheritance tax
- Planning for school fees
- Action on family breakdown

Protecting the family

Financial provision
This is usually the most important objective for the head of a family since he will wish to ensure that others are well provided for in the event of his being unable to maintain them through death or disability. Often this provision is through life assurance, but it is important to make sure that the financial provision is wrapped up in a tax effective way.

Life assurance:
Effecting life assurance policies can be the most straightforward way of protecting the family in the event of the death of the breadwinner. These could be term assurance policies (providing a lump sum or an income in the event of death within a fixed period of time, eg before retirement) or longer term endowment or whole of life policies which may also provide an investment return.

Tax effectiveness:
Policies are often left solely for the benefit of the surviving spouse who is then given the responsibility of looking after the children. A more tax effective way, maximising the benefits available for the family, could be to arrange for part of the insurance benefits to arise in a simple trust fund which would meet the costs of maintaining and educating the children. This can often give rise to income tax savings of up to £677 pa for each child.

Permanent health insurance:
This will insure you against the possibility of becoming unable to work for prolonged periods. Statistics show that a man of 45 is many times more likely to become unable to work for a year or more before he retires than he is to die before then. Permanent health insurance provides an income during prolonged periods of illness or disability and the income is often not subject to tax until it has been paid for at least 12 months.

Wills

If you have not made a will, on your death your assets will be distributed in accordance with the laws of intestacy and this may result in some people benefiting contrary to your own intentions.

> *Example: John and Cathy have been married for five years and jointly own a house valued at £50,000 with a £25,000 mortgage protected by a life assurance policy. Additionally, each of them has a life policy which will pay out £20,000 in the event of their deaths. John has also been paying contributions to a pension plan and this would be worth £10,000 on his death. They have no children.*
>
> *If John was killed in an accident and Cathy died shortly afterwards, the whole of their estate of £100,000 (ie house, plus life policies, plus pension) would pass back to Cathy's parents under the laws of intestacy. If her parents were not alive, the capital would be divided among her brothers and sisters.*
>
> *This may be particularly undesirable if, for example, Cathy's parents were already fairly wealthy or if John's family were in financial difficulty.*

Consequently, it is very important to ensure that you have made a valid will which sets down your intentions. It is also important to make sure that this is kept up to date to cater for changing personal and family circumstances.

Divorce now automatically revokes clauses in a will making bequests to an ex-spouse or appointing the ex-spouse executor/trustee, unless a contrary intention is clear from the will itself. In any event, divorce usually involves a major rearrangement of the couple's wealth and the previous wills may be inappropriate.

It is usually wise to include a clause in a will providing that assets will pass to a surviving spouse only if he or she survives the deceased by a month. This covers the possibility of both being involved in an accident. No IHT problems will arise if the survivorship period does not exceed six months.

In drafting a will, some fairly substantial inheritance tax savings can often be made by including a few straightforward provisions. See *Mitigating Inheritance Tax* (page 32).

Minimising income tax

Many income tax savings can be made by simple planning so that you take full advantage of the various exemptions and reliefs. For example:

Company cars

If you are a director or an employee earning over £8,500 pa, the benefit of a company car is taxed according to a scale. The scale charge depends on the original market value, engine capacity and age of the car. This scale benefit is halved if business mileage in this tax year exceeds 18,000. On the other hand, if business use is less than 2,500 miles (or if the car is a second company car), the scale charge is increased by 50%.

In borderline cases, you should consider bringing forward business trips to ensure that the mileage thresholds are reached by 5 April.

Any fuel provided by your employer for your private use will be taxed on a separate fixed scale irrespective of the quantity of fuel supplied. Consequently, you should reconsider whether it is worthwhile being given fuel for private use, bearing in mind that the tax charge may now exceed the benefit received.

Wife's earnings

A working wife can earn up to £2,335 (1986/87) before being liable to pay any income tax on her earnings (although it should be remembered that she will become liable to national insurance contributions on her earnings if these are in excess of £38.00 per week). Consequently, if the wife works for her husband's business it may be worthwhile arranging for an appropriate salary to be paid to her. Furthermore, this would allow the provision of tax efficient pension benefits.

If a husband and wife are both working, separate taxation of wife's earnings should be considered. For 1986/87, the minimum joint earned income for this to become beneficial is £26,520. Of this, the spouse earning the lower amount should have an income of at least £6,986. An election must be made by 5 April 1988 in respect of earnings in 1986/87. This time limit is extended for two years in respect of members of Lloyd's. An election for separate taxation of 1985/86 earnings can also be made before 5 April 1987. For that year, the minimum joint earned income for this to become beneficial was £25,360, with the lower paid spouse earning at least £6,955. These figures are given after mortgage interest, covenants etc.

If the wife is working and the husband is not and has no other income, then the wife can obtain the benefit of the married man's personal tax allowance (1986/87; £3,655) as well as the wife's earned income relief bringing her total tax allowances up to £5,990.

If the wife has earnings but does not belong to an employer's pension scheme, then she should consider making contributions to a personal pension plan in order to obtain tax relief and generate an earned income after retirement. Although this is extremely tax efficient, in some cases it may be necessary to restrict the amount contributed to a plan to ensure that tax relief is not wasted by reducing the net amount to less than the wife's earned income relief limit.

Tax deferral – industrial buildings

If you have a particularly high income, some of your tax liabilities may be deferred by investing in woodlands, or the Business Expansion Scheme or an Enterprise Zone building. See Part 3.

Minor children

Children under 18 are entitled to claim a personal tax allowance and can therefore receive income of up to £2,335 pa free of tax. However, income arising on cash or assets gifted by a parent is, in most cases, still treated as that of the parent for tax purposes, unless made under a court order. This means that gifts from parents should normally be invested in assets which produce no income in order to avoid aggregation.

However, there is one situation in which income arising on investments gifted by a parent is not aggregated with the parent's income. This is where the income is accumulated in a bare trust for the child without being *paid or applied* for his benefit until he reaches 18. Provided the income arising is not used, in any way, for the child's benefit until after the child's eighteenth birthday, the income can effectively accumulate tax free within the child's tax allowance.

Deeds of covenant can be an effective method of transferring income to a minor child where the donor is someone other than a parent, perhaps a grandparent or other relative, for example.

Students

It is becoming increasingly popular for parents of students aged 18 or over to make payments to them under covenant whilst they are undergoing full time education. The legislation requires payments under such covenants to be capable of exceeding six years – hence the normal seven year period – but it is possible for the covenant to terminate earlier in certain circumstances. Many covenants provide for payment over a seven year period, or until the beneficiary ceases to undergo full time education if sooner. The Inland revenue has now published a draft Deed of Covenant for this purpose in leaflet IR47.

In some circumstances, the covenant can be for a variable sum (defined at the outset), such as an amount equal to the personal tax allowance for the year. Normally, covenanted payments are ignored by a local authority when calculating student grants but, if the parents are separated or if the student qualifies for an independent grant, the grant could be reduced.

The existence of a covenant may affect eligibility for unemployment benefit. Any benefit which is received is now taxable and this will absorb part of the student's personal tax allowance.

Woodlands
Woodlands can be a very tax efficient way of investing capital or of accumulating capital from income. From the income tax point of view, the planting and maintenance costs of commercial woodlands can be set against a taxpayer's general income. Relief can also be claimed for capital expenditure on new fences, roads, buildings and drainage work.

Charities
Many people make regular donations to charity, but overlook the fact that tax advantages could be obtained by using a deed of covenant.

For tax relief to be obtained on a covenant to a charity, the payments must be capable of exceeding three years. In practice this means four covenanted payments. The gross amount of payments due after 5 April 1986 under covenants to charities will be deductible for the purposes of higher rates of tax.

If you wish to benefit a number of different charities or to vary the charities each year, it is possible to route covenanted payments through a charitable body such as the Charities Aid Foundation which will distribute to charities of your choice. Alternatively, you may establish your own charitable trust.

Provided all the funds are either distributed for charitable purposes or accumulated to pay out later to charity, the anti-avoidance provisions within Finance Act 1986 should not apply.

From 5 April 1987, tax relief will also be available where an employee pays up to £100 each year under a payroll deduction scheme operated by his employer.

Minimising capital gains tax

Husband and wife
Gains and losses of a husband and wife are calculated separately for each spouse, losses being set off primarily against gains of that spouse before the totals are aggregated. Where one spouse has net gains of less than £6,300 (1986/87) and the other spouse net losses it may be advantageous to elect for the losses to be isolated. The net losses of the one spouse are then carried forward to subsequent years instead of being set off in the current year against the gains of the other. An election must be made by 6 July in the year following the year of assessment and relates to all subsequent years until it is withdrawn.

Private residence relief
It is well known that the gain on disposal by an individual of his private residence is exempt from capital gains tax. There are, however, a number of planning points which should be borne in mind if this relief is to be maximised:

- Avoid selling the property in separate parcels. If only part of a garden is sold with a dwelling house any subsequent sale of the retained land will not qualify for relief.
- Where any part of a dwelling house is used exclusively for business purposes, that part will not qualify for relief. However, provided no part of the house is used *exclusively* for business purposes, full relief should still be available.
- From 6 April 1980 relief is available for the disposal of a person's principal private residence if any part of it has been let as residential accommodation at any time during the period of ownership. Any gain arising on a disposal is reduced by the lower of the relief attributable to owner occupation or £20,000 (£10,000 prior to 6 April 1983).

Second residences
Where an individual owns two or more properties, he may elect which is to be treated as his main residence to attract CGT exemption. The exemption then applies to the period during which

the election is in force and to the final two years of ownership in any event.

Someone who owns two houses may be able to reduce his CGT on the second house, simply by electing for it to be treated as his main residence for a few days, since this will mean that the last two years of ownership will also be exempt. Even if he owns it for more than two years, this could ensure that part of the gain is tax free.

It is worthwhile considering an election on purchase of a second residence as the Revenue's view is that an election must be made within two years from the acquisition of any residence. However, authority for this view is difficult to find in the legislation.

Retirement relief

You do not need to retire before claiming retirement relief from capital gains tax. It is sufficient that you are over 60 and disposing of the whole or part of a business or shares in a family trading company. The relief extends to a maximum gain of £100,000 for each of a husband and wife.

There is now a general hold-over relief for gifts made by individuals and trustees. When coupled with retirement relief, it may be possible to transfer, say, shares in a family trading company to the next generation, paying no capital gains tax. The younger generation would inherit a cost significantly increased by retirement relief. This could be important in any future disposal by the younger generation.

Trusts

Trusts have the benefit of an annual CGT exemption of up to £3,150. However, where one settlor has made a number of settlements (other than non resident or charitable trusts, or trusts for the mentally disabled) after 6 June 1978, the £3,150 exemption is divided by the number of such settlements, subject to a minimum exemption of £630 per settlement. Trustees should consider realising gains each year to utilise the exemption.

If both a husband and wife create separate settlements, then the settlements created by each of them will benefit from the £3,150 exemption.

Sales at an undervalue

The general relief for gifts can be used to take advantage of the donor's annual CGT exemption. For example, the donor could arrange to sell an asset at an undervalue calculated to leave him with a gain of £6,300 (or some smaller or larger figure to take advantage of his exemption and losses in the year).

31

Non resident trusts

The establishment of settlements with non resident trustees is very attractive in certain circumstances. Non resident trustees may not be liable to pay UK capital gains tax and gains may therefore accumulate gross within the trust. UK beneficiaries will suffer CGT only when capital payments are made to them. This means that liabilities to CGT may be deferred almost indefinitely.

It is not possible to hold over gains when settling on non resident trustees, but consideration might be given to the creation of a UK trust with a view to 'exporting' it before realising gains. Any capital gain then accruing *after* creation of the settlement may arise tax free to the then non resident trustees.

Consideration should also be given to appointing non resident trustees to existing settlements where possible. To avoid a CGT charge, this should be done well before 5 April preceding a disposal of the assets. This is a complex area and detailed advice should be sought.

Creation of an overseas settlement may also provide some protection in the event of a reintroduction of exchange controls in the UK. The income tax position of overseas trustees can be quite complicated for both the trustees and beneficiaries and must be considered carefully.

Mitigating inheritance tax (IHT)

Often the most dramatic savings can come from one or two simple steps which do not involve complex arrangements and extensive costs. For example:

Pension death benefits

Many employers' pension schemes provide for a lump sum to be paid to an employee's family or dependants on his death. Most commonly, a husband nominates this in favour of his wife since she will, of course, require an income to support her and may need access to the underlying capital.

However, it can be far more tax effective to create a simple 'pilot' trust and then to request that any pension scheme death benefits be paid into this trust. The widow and family would be beneficiaries of the fund and the income can be paid back to the widow in exactly the same way as if she had received and invested the capital herself. However, it will not form part of her estate for IHT purposes and so will not bear tax on her subsequent death. There can also be income tax savings of up to £677 per annum for each minor child left by the husband.

Similar arrangements are possible for individuals who do not belong to an employer's pension scheme but who have been making payments to a personal pension plan.

Life policies

Similarly, most life policies are held by a husband and wife so that the survivor of them will benefit from the proceeds. This means that the proceeds will eventually bear IHT when the survivor dies. It is therefore advantageous to transfer the benefit of the policies to the type of trust mentioned above so that the survivor can benefit from the use of the capital but without it actually forming part of the estate for IHT purposes.

Reversionary interests

Where an individual has a reversionary interest in a trust fund (for example, if he expects to receive the capital of the fund on the death of another beneficiary) that interest may be given away without attracting any IHT liability. In this way, large sums of capital can move through generations free of IHT. Consideration should be given to disposing of reversionary interests, either by giving them away completely or by transferring them into a new trust fund.

Wills

Substantial savings can often be made by including appropriate provisions in a will. For example:

Nil rate band:
Instead of a husband leaving all his assets to his wife on his death, he could arrange for the sum of £71,000 (or the then nil-rate band) to pass to a discretionary trust under which his wife would be the primary beneficiary. As with the trusts set out above, the wife could receive income and capital from the trust but it would not ultimately suffer IHT on her death. This can give rise to IHT savings of up to £42,600.

Business relief:
Business property is favourably treated for IHT purposes since it can be discounted in value by up to 50%. Often, however, this relief is wasted since business property is left to a surviving spouse (this transfer is exempt from tax) and the survivor then realises the assets or sells the business so that she receives cash which then qualifies for no relief. In these circumstances, it is much better to arrange for the business property to pass to a trust fund from which the survivor can

benefit. This is particularly appropriate for underwriting members of Lloyd's.

Lifetime gifts

Transferring large amounts of capital (in excess of the exemptions) during one's lifetime gives rise to three tax advantages:

- Capital growth can accrue tax free outside the donor's estate, rather than inside where it will simply aggravate his IHT position.
- Chargeable transfers will be 'written off' for tax purposes after seven years allowing further transfers to be made.
- Outright gifts in excess of the nil–rate band will only attract tax if the donor fails to survive for seven years, and if the donor survives for from three to seven years the tax charge is reduced.

If appropriate, term assurance cover could be effected to cover the additional tax liabilities which might arise on death within the three or seven year periods.

Using IHT exemptions

Substantial IHT savings can be made by making systematic use of the available exemptions.

It is essential to ensure that, wherever possible, the exemptions are utilised to the full each year.

It is possible to use the spouse exemption, £3,000 annual exemption and marriage exemption to reduce the tax liability on the coming to an end (or reduction) of an 'interest in possession' in settled (trust) property. This means that people who receive income from trusts may consider partially realising their interests in order to utilise these exemptions.

'Off the shelf' products

A large number of life assurance companies formerly marketed CTT planning products which fell into two separate categories: inheritance trusts and discounted gift plans. These were very worthwhile in some circumstances, but it was necessary to invest a cash sum, and this could mean incurring a capital gains tax liability, eg if you had to sell shares to make the investment. See Part 3 for further details. Most of these schemes were withdrawn immediately after the 1986 Budget Statement but they may reappear in a revised form. In most cases, arrangements set up before the Budget will continue to be tax effective.

Using loans
Loans can be an effective way of reducing IHT liabilities, but there are some anti-avoidance provisions to be considered.

Interest free loans:
It is possible to make interest free loans without any IHT liability arising.

Index-linked loans:
Where an individual is borrowing capital, instead of paying a high rate of interest on a fixed capital sum outstanding, he should consider a loan where the capital sum is index-linked. Apart from reducing his interest outgoings, this will increase the debt on his estate to be deducted before calculating his overall IHT liability on his death. There are provisions to prevent the avoidance of tax through certain loans back to the original donor.

Favourably treated property
Certain types of property are favourably treated under the inheritance tax legislation.

Woodlands:
The value of any growing timber (not the land on which it grows) may be omitted from an individual's estate at death. IHT will not become payable until a subsequent disposal of the timber by the person who inherited it. There are other conditions attaching to the relief but the overall effect is to postpone tax.

National heritage property:
This covers property of great scientific, historic or artistic interest, and certain types of land and buildings. There is a conditional exemption for transfers, whether during lifetime or on death. Furthermore, a gift of national heritage property to museums, art galleries and the like may be exempt from IHT.

Agricultural and business property:
These qualify for a relief which is given against the value of the property. The rate of relief is either 50% or 30% of the value of the property. There are many conditions attaching to these reliefs and it should be remembered that the two reliefs can overlap, as will often be the case with working farmers.

Instalments

On a transfer of land or certain business property where the recipient agrees to pay the tax, the liability may be spread over ten years by annual instalments, often interest free. One advantage of the instalment method is that the transfer will have a lower value for IHT than if the donor had paid the tax, and consequently the tax will be less. Furthermore, the donor could fund the annual instalments out of his annual exemptions or, perhaps, by the exemption applicable to normal·expenditure out of income, if he wished.

The option to pay by instalments will not apply where a potentially exempt transfer becomes chargeable and the donee no longer owns the asset.

Using the home

If your home is your only major asset, we usually recommend that it is not used in tax planning arrangements since your emotional and financial security is usually far more important than possible tax savings.

Where the house is to be used in IHT planning, it is sometimes suggested that part of the house is left directly to the family on the death of the first parent. Although this can be effective, it is fraught with legal, taxation and commercial problems.

A preferable way of dealing with the problem is to leave the house in the ownership of the couple, but to reduce its value by encumbering it with a mortgage of up to £30,000. Provided the couple are aged 65 or over, the interest they pay on the mortgage will qualify for full income tax relief provided that the £30,000 raised is used to purchase an annuity. The annuity payments can then be used to service the interest on the mortgage and to pay the premiums to a life assurance contract written under trust for the benefit of the family. The sum assured is usually at least equal to the loan so that the family's capital, as a whole, is protected but up to £30,000 avoids an IHT charge.

It is essential that, if you are contemplating a home income/IHT plan, you seek professional advice, particularly following the introduction of certain anti-avoidance provisions.

Two-year discretionary trusts

If in your will you leave your estate to a discretionary trust, assets distributed from the trust within two years of death suffer IHT and CGT as if you had made the bequests in your will. Your spouse is usually made a trustee and you can note your wishes in a letter which can be revised without formalities at any time. A discretionary will trust is therefore a very flexible and tax efficient way of making sure that your estate is distributed in the most appropriate way.

When trying to minimise IHT by making full use of the nil and lower rate bands of tax on the first death, it is never easy to estimate the financial needs of the survivor. A discretionary will trust obviates the need to make this decision prior to death and allows a period of two years for thought. Maximum possible flexibility is given to deal with the estate in the light of the legislation applicable at the time of death and the financial circumstances of all members of the family.

A similar result can be achieved by using a deed of variation (see below) but this is not so flexible. The main advantage of a discretionary trust over a deed of variation is that there is no need to obtain agreement from the original beneficiaries. Furthermore, if a parent gives up a legacy in favour of a minor child, under a deed of variation this is likely to give rise to income tax problems which do not arise under a discretionary trust.

Deeds of variation

In the last resort, provided all beneficiaries are of age and sound mind, they may execute a deed varying the will of a deceased person within two years of death. In this event, IHT will be payable as if the deceased had executed the will in the rewritten form.

A deed of variation allows a family to reconsider the distribution of the deceased's estate in line with both the needs of the family as a whole and relevant taxation provisions. Although this can be very helpful, for practical as well as taxation reasons, this is not as flexible as a two year discretionary trust (see above) since any beneficiary who is giving up part of his benefit under the will must give his consent and this is not possible where minor beneficiaries are involved.

Planning for school fees

General

The high cost of private education has made it necessary for most people to plan ahead to meet school fee commitments. Advance provision may be made either from income or capital or from a combination of the two. Such provisions can be aimed at meeting fees on a level or increasing basis.

In practice it is difficult to make provision for the full amount of anticipated fees of a chosen school so it becomes necessary to top up out of income when the fees become payable.

Income funding

Advance funding out of income is usually satisfactory if arrangements are established in good time, a number of years before the fees are required. Typical investments might include regular purchases of National Savings Certificates or saving through unit trusts or life assurance policies. The new Personal Equity Plans may also be appropriate. See Part 3.

Capital funding

Capital funding is usually more suitable where school fees are required within the near future, say five years, or where adequate capital resources are available for this purpose. Possible investment areas include a series of low coupon gilt-edged securities. Alternatively, specialist school fees plans, based around charitable educational trusts, are available.

Some schools also offer arrangements under which a capital sum is paid in advance of future fees. Depending on the details of the scheme, this can give a tax free, inflation-proofed return.

When considering capital funding it is important to establish who is providing the capital: if it is provided by a parent, there ought to be no inheritance tax problems.

Income tax

Where a sum is paid out of a trust to meet school fees, the Inland Revenue may contend that this should be taxed as income, irrespective of whether it has been paid from trust income or capital. This might be avoided if a single payment is made out of capital directly to a third party such as a school.

Action on family breakdown

Maintenance payments

In most circumstances, a husband will be required to support his former wife and children by regular income payments (although sometimes the wife can be required to support her former husband). In either event, some important tax benefits can be obtained by structuring this in the correct way.

The following points assume that the children reside with the mother who is receiving – not paying - maintenance:

Court order:
Rather than making voluntary payments (which have no tax effect: payments neither attract relief in the payer's hands nor are taxed in

the recipient's) it can be advantageous to make maintenance payments under a formal agreement. This means that the payer obtains tax relief and the recipient suffers tax (but often at a lower rate).

It is possible for a court order to be back-dated so that these tax benefits are obtained on what were voluntary payments, but the order cannot be back-dated to before the original application to the court and both parties must agree to this. Furthermore, there must have been no undue delay by the parties in pressing the application.

Children:

Where payments are made under a court order, it is advantageous to arrange for part of the maintenance payments to be made directly to the children rather than to the mother since this will reduce the amount of tax payable. No tax will be payable by the children if each receives maintenance payments of not more than the single person's allowance assuming this to be the child's only income.

If the children are under 21 and the payments are for their benefit, maintenance or education, then no tax need be deducted on making the payments provided they do not exceed £48 per week or £208 per month. There can therefore be a substantial cash flow advantage in ensuring that the payments do not exceed these amounts, otherwise separate claims will have to be made to the Inland Revenue each year for the tax deducted to be refunded.

School fees:

If you wish to incorporate school fees in the maintenance arrangements for tax purposes, it is essential to obtain a court order to prevent the arrangement being treated as a settlement. The courts have no jurisdiction to order payment of school fees as such. The order should, therefore, require the father to pay additional maintenance. The amount of this should be a sum calculated on the basis that, after tax has been paid, sufficient cash will be available to pay the school fees. The father must not be contractually liable to the school for payment of the fees.

The Inland Revenue like to see special standard documentation which includes a contract between the child and the school and an appointment of the school bursar as the child's agent. A recent court case has highlighted the need to take great care in this area.

Bills:

In some cases, the divorce or separation agreement may provide that the husband must meet his wife's household or living expenses. This is not effective for tax purposes and it is usually preferable to arrange for this type of agreement to be amended and for the contractual maintenance to be increased accordingly.

Family home

Both parties will need a home after the separation and it may be necessary to pay for both of them out of the one income which formerly provided for just one home. Tax points on MIRAS and CGT should be borne in mind:

MIRAS:

If the husband is responsible for paying the mortgage on his former wife's property, the amount of tax relief he can claim on a new property for himself will be greatly reduced. It is therefore usually worthwhile arranging for the former wife to take over the mortgage on the first house and receive correspondingly increased maintenance payments. This will then allow the husband to obtain full tax relief on a new mortgage of up to £30,000 to fund his new home.

Capital gains tax:

If the husband continues to own a share of the matrimonial home, he can potentially be liable to capital gains tax when it is eventually sold. One way around this is to transfer his interest in the property to his former wife.

National insurance

From the date of the decree absolute, a woman has to pay full rate national insurance contributions if she is working, even if she previously paid at the reduced rate. A certain number of national insurance contributions must be paid to qualify for benefits such as unemployment benefit and the basic retirement pension. However, in certain circumstances a divorced woman can use her ex-husband's contribution record to qualify for a retirement pension if it is better than her own.

Detailed advice should be taken on the overall national insurance position.

Inheritance tax

The crucial date as regards the application of IHT to transfers between spouses is the date of the decree absolute. Transfers between the spouses prior to the decree absolute are exempt from IHT, provided both are domiciled in the UK. After this time, this exemption ceases to apply and transfers between the former spouses can be liable to IHT in the ordinary way. There are, however, two statutory exemptions which can be relevant.

No 'gratuitous benefit':
A transfer of capital is not taxable if it is not intended to confer gratuitous benefit and is broadly at the commercial price. The Inland Revenue agree that this exemption will cover transfers of property pursuant to orders of the Divorce Court.

Transfers for maintenance:
A transfer of capital is not taxable if it is made by a husband for his former wife (or vice versa) for her maintenance, or to his children provided that it is for their maintenance, education or training.

Wills
It is essential that wills are fully reviewed.

Executors:
It is common practice where a husband and wife make wills for each to appoint the other as executor, or trustee, of the will. When the marriage is dissolved or annulled those appointments will cease to have effect and both parties should reconsider the appointment of executors.

Bequests:
Divorce automatically disinherits the spouse unless the wording of the will specifically states that the bequest can still be made.

Reconsideration:
Separation or divorce should prompt a full reconsideration of the provisions of the will. The assets of the individual parties change on marriage breakdown and there may also be a change in the identity of beneficiaries. Great care must be taken to ensure that the children and other dependents are adequately provided for following the death of either spouse.

Pension death benefits:
Although this is not usually dealt with in a will, an individual may usually nominate the beneficiary to whom he would like any death benefits from his employer's pension scheme to be paid. Clearly, if a nomination has been made this should be reviewed. From the inheritance tax point of view, it is usually worthwhile nominating the benefit to a 'pilot' trust.

41

Life assurance

Both parties should review all policies they hold to consider whether any changes are necessary. Some policies may be considered unnecessary and others may have to be rearranged to fit the new circumstances.

Where tax relief is available on policies which were taken out prior to March 1984, it is particularly worthwhile reviewing the position in order to ensure that relief can continue.

Chapter 5
Planning for Retirement

This breaks down into three separate areas:

- Preparing for retirement
- Decisions at retirement
- Investing in retirement

Preparing for retirement

Pensions

Pension arrangements approved by the Inland Revenue offer the most tax efficient way of providing for an income after retirement. In broad terms:

- contributions to a pension plan are eligible for tax relief;
- investments are made in a fund which suffers no tax on income or capital gains;
- at retirement, part of the accumulated fund may be taken as a tax-free lump sum.

Employers can establish company pension schemes and many individuals can effect personal pension plans (PPPs). These two types of pension are governed by very different tax rules. Basically, under a company scheme there are strict limits on the benefits which can be paid out of the scheme, but under a PPP there are limits on the amount which can be paid in.

Personal pension plans

A self-employed person or an employee who is not a member of a company pension scheme may contribute to a personal pension plan. Contributions of up to 17.5% (more for those born before 1934) of your net earnings from the occupation will attract full tax relief. This will normally reduce your tax liability in the tax year in which the contribution is made. The following points should be borne in mind:

- contributions may be related back to the previous tax year (or, in certain circumstances, two years) to that of payment. This might maximise the tax relief available. In this event an election

must be made not later than 5 July following the tax year of payment;
- special rules apply to Lloyd's underwriters (see below);
- it is possible to pay contributions in excess of the 17.5% limit if less than the maximum has been paid in previous years.

In order to obtain these tax reliefs, it is not normally possible to draw benefits from a pension plan before age 60. However, most companies offer a 'loanback' arrangement under which they will lend monies to the policyholder, at a commercial rate and with collateral security, without requiring evidence of financial status or enquiring as to the purpose of the loan. This can free money which would otherwise be locked into a pension plan (see below).

Company schemes
Any company can establish a pension scheme for the benefit of its employees, including any shareholding directors. This can be an extremely tax efficient way of drawing company profits. Full tax relief is available on contributions to a pension scheme.

Employee contributions:
An employee who is a member of a company pension scheme may normally contribute to the scheme up to 15% of his total earnings from the employment. Provided such contributions are made on a regular basis (ie over at least five years) tax relief at the employee's highest rate may be obtained.

Most schemes allow for an employee to pay additional voluntary contributions (AVC's) which will qualify for tax relief as set out above. These can be invested in a variety of ways, but are most commonly invested in a building society account (where interest is added without any tax being deducted) or in a life assurance pension arrangement. At retirement, the accumulated fund can be paid out tax free (within the Revenue limits) or can be used to increase the individual's pension entitlement. See Part 3.

Company contributions:
Company payments to a pension scheme attract full tax relief. Contributions cannot be backdated for tax relief purposes except for Lloyd's agencies (see below). This is particularly relevant where a company may consider making a special contribution.

Job changers' options
If an individual leaves a job having accumulated pension rights, there are usually four ways in which his pension benefits can be dealt with:

Refund of contributions:
If he has worked for the company for less than five years, he can often obtain a refund of his personal contributions to the scheme (perhaps with interest), but subject to a flat rate tax deduction of 10%.

Deferred pension:
His basic entitlement will be to a deferred pension from his former employer which will be payable at the normal retirement date. Usually, this pension will be frozen in value, although any benefits which have accrued since 1 January 1985 must be increased by up to 5% per annum.

Transfer value:
Instead of retaining a deferred pension with the old employer, pension schemes now have to offer the alternative of a transfer to another pension scheme. In this way, a lump sum will be paid across to a new company pension scheme and this may result in a higher pension for the individual.

Transfer plan:
Instead of taking the transfer value into another pension scheme, the individual can, subject to a number of conditions, arrange for the transfer value to be paid into an insurance based pension contract which may offer the prospect of better benefits. This is a contract directly between the individual and the insurance company and so he will receive the full benefit of it even if he changes jobs again in the future.

Investing for retirement
Apart from approved pension arrangements, there are no investments specifically aimed at providing for retirement, but many conventional investments can nevertheless be very worthwhile.

Saving out of income:
You should consider:

- Personal Equity Plans;
- Maximum Investment Plans;
- National Savings Yearly Plan;
- Unit Trust Savings Plans.

45

Investing existing capital:
It is usually more important to invest for capital gains (and thereby increased future income) than it is to invest for current income. Consider

- unit trusts for capital growth;
- investment bonds;
- low coupon gilts, etc;
- off-shore roll-up funds;
- zero coupon bonds.

Decisions at retirement

Retirement date
Your exact retirement date can often make a substantial difference to your pension benefits. For example:

- company pension schemes often base benefits on an employee's earnings on a set date, or in the previous calendar year. In this case retiring on, for example, 31 December could mean that your pension is lower than if you had retired a day later on 1 January;
- with-profit pension policies attract bonuses which are usually based on policies in force on 31 December in the previous year. Often this means that it is better to cash in a policy on 1 January rather than 30 December, and in one recent case this resulted in an overall increase in benefits of 16%.

Pension options
It is often necessary to make decisions at retirement about the way in which pension benefits will be drawn. Commonly there is the right to commute part of the pension for a tax free lump sum. There may also be the option to draw a reduced pension, and to provide for widow's benefits and some increases in the future to off-set the effects of inflation. Whilst the right approach will depend upon your personal circumstances, the following points might be borne in mind:

Pension commutation:
It is usually worthwhile commuting as much pension as possible into tax-free cash at the time of retirement. This is because the cash can, for example, be used to buy an annuity which will generally provide at least as good a pension as could have been drawn originally, but part is tax free.

If you do not need a high pension immediately, the lump sum can be invested for capital growth so that it can be drawn upon to supplement the pension in future, as required.

Widow's benefits:
It is usually important to make sure that a widow continues to receive pension benefits for her lifetime, although this is obviously less important if there are substantial investments available to support her. Ideally, there should be a pension payable to her in her own right.

Pension increases:
Over the last ten years, inflation has averaged over 9.7% per annum so that a fixed pension of £1,000 per annum in March 1976 would be worth only £395 pa in today's terms. There should, therefore, be some provision for the pension to increase in the future. One or two insurance companies now offer fully index-linked annuities but these are very expensive.

Open market options:
Where a pension fund has been built up with an insurance company, it is often possible to uplift the accumulated fund and buy the pension itself from another insurance company. This can sometimes be very advantageous since some companies are competitive on investment returns, whilst others are more competitive on annuity payments.

Golden handshakes
There are special rules for taxing termination payments when someone leaves an employment. Amounts up to £25,000 are usually exempt from tax; amounts over £25,000 and up to £75,000 suffer a reduced rate of tax. Payments may also be made to a pension fund without tax. Care should be taken to avoid any payment being treated as an emolument from the employment and therefore fully taxable. Another trap to avoid is having the payment treated as part of the consideration an individual receives for any disposal of his shares.

It is also important that the payer obtains relief. The tax law is fairly complicated, so professional advice should be obtained at an early stage.

Maturing endowments
Many people arrange their finances around their expected retirement date. A mortgage is often repaid and endowment policies mature at this time.

47

Instead of taking the proceeds of a maturing endowment policy as a lump sum in cash, it is often preferable to leave the proceeds invested with the insurance company. The funds can then be drawn upon whenever capital is required, but in the meanwhile it will continue to grow in value free of any personal tax liability. Furthermore, a tax free income can be drawn out of the policy.

Consequently, where an endowment policy has been linked to a mortgage, it is often worthwhile considering repaying the mortgage from other resources so that a larger sum is left invested with the life company.

Age allowance

Someone aged 65 or over will benefit from an increased personal tax allowance provided that his total income does not exceed £9,400 gross for 1986/87. Above this limit, the allowance is gradually reduced to the normal personal allowance and in this band income is effectively taxed at about 50%. Where total income exceeds £10,173 (single person) or £10,675 (married couple), the allowance ceases to be effective. Wherever possible this tax band should be avoided, if necessary by rearranging investments.

Investing in retirement

Objectives

The most appropriate investments will depend entirely on the circumstances of the individuals concerned. Some difficult decisions need to be made. For example, should a high income be drawn today at the expense of a reduced income (in real and, perhaps, monetary terms) in the future? How accessible does the capital need to be? Can I afford to take some risks, or should I stick with some 'safe' investments? With inflation continuing, can I afford not to take risks?

Annuities

For those requiring a very high level of immediate income, annuities can be considered. This involves paying capital to an insurance company in exchange for an income which will be payable throughout your lifetime. The annuity normally ceases on your death, although it could be guaranteed to be payable for a minimum period (to account for the possibility of your dying in the immediate future) or it could be payable whilst either you or your wife is alive. The annuity may be of a level amount or it may increase at a specified rate each year. Index-linked annuities are also available, as are property linked annuities under which the annuity payments will reflect the investment return on property.

In each case, part of the annuity will be free of tax (as a return of capital) and part will be taxed as investment income.

For those wishing to conserve capital, the following investments might be considered:

	Objective		
Investment	**Current Income**	**Growing Income**	**Capital Growth**
Gilts and fixed interest securities	☆	☆	☆
Index-linked gilts		☆	☆
Building Society	☆		
Guaranteed bonds	☆		☆
National Savings Income Bonds	☆		
National Savings Certificates			☆
Unit Trusts	☆	☆	☆
Investment bonds	☆	☆	☆
Equity portfolio		☆	☆
Zero coupon bonds			☆
Offshore money funds			☆

Please see Part 3 for further information on each investment area.

Chapter 6

Planning for Businessmen

Financial planning for a businessman can involve:

- Income tax planning (for the self-employed)
- Corporation tax planning
- Capital gains tax planning
- National insurance contribution planning

Income tax planning

Pensions

Approved pension arrangements provide the most tax effective way of setting aside business profits to provide for a future income.

Frequently, a businessman is reluctant to set aside substantial sums for pension provision since he may feel that he is better able to use the money himself. However, there are now two opportunities for unlocking pension funds:

Self-administered PPPs:

Some insurance companies will allow the investor in a personal pension plan to establish and run his own investment fund, subject to a number of conditions. This is appropriate where fairly large sums are involved, perhaps £20,000 or more. In certain circumstances the fund may invest back in the business by, for example, buying the property out of which the business operates.

Loanbacks:

A recent development is the concept of raising finance linked to a person's pension benefits. The insurance company lends the amount of capital in the individual's pension fund against the security of other assets. This loan would bear a commercial rate of interest, but the insurance company, subject to a service charge, would then credit this to his pension fund. The loan would be repaid out of part of the tax-free cash sum from the pension benefits at retirement.

An extension of this is to borrow capital from an independent finance company. The sum borrowed is often expressed as a multiple of the contributions to a pension arrangement. The advantage of this facility is the ability to make payments of interest with the capital being repaid out of the lump sum retirement benefits. Needless to say, the ultimate repayment can significantly reduce the individual's remaining pension benefits.

This approach is often suggested for financing house purchase as an alternative to a repayment or endowment based mortgage. It can be attractive where the borrower is paying high rates of tax, but it is necessary to look at costs and benefits separately in each case.

A point to bear in mind is that you are rarely obliged to draw on private pension benefits at the official retirement date. In some cases the benefits can be substantially increased by delaying taking the benefits until the next bonus declaration or unit prices pick up.

Instant low-cost pensions:
Personal pension plans are often regarded as irrelevant for older people even though they may be high rate taxpayers who are eligible to pay sizeable contributions. In these circumstances however, the plans can be exceptionally efficient.

> *Example: A man aged 74 who pays tax at 60% is eligible to pay £10,000 into a pension plan. A single contribution of this amount will cost him £4,000 after tax relief.*
>
> *If he were to retire immediately, a pension of approximately £1,050 per annum would be receivable throughout his lifetime and, in addition, he could withdraw a tax free cash sum of approximately £3,400. His pension of £1,050 per annum has cost only £600 net.*

Interest relief

In general, interest paid on borrowings to fund a business qualifies for income tax relief, whilst that on borrowings for personal expenditure (including purchase of a house with a mortgage of more than £30,000) does not qualify for tax relief. Frequently, it is possible to rearrange borrowings in a more tax-effective way. For example, it may be possible to draw capital out of a business to repay non-allowable borrowings and then to borrow, on a tax allowable basis, to fund the increased cash needs of the business.

There are a number of pitfalls in this and detailed advice should be sought.

Wife

Where a wife works for a business it is appropriate to pay her a commercial salary and this can result in tax savings. Furthermore, this then allows pension provision to be made in respect of her salary, provided that the salary is a tax allowable expense for the employer. The pension contributions will attract tax relief in the usual way.

It is sometimes possible to make tax allowable pension contributions of amounts in excess of her salary and, apart from the availability of a tax-free cash sum at retirement, the pension will be taxed as her own earned income. It will therefore qualify for wife's earned income relief and may be tax free.

Where a wife plays a significant part in the business, it may be worthwhile considering making her a partner in it since this may allow a larger part of the profit to be apportioned to her than if she were an employee.

In any event, the costs and benefits of national insurance must be considered.

Corporation tax planning

Wife

If you run your business through a company, it can still be worthwhile paying a salary to your wife in respect of work done by her. Tax allowable pension contributions can then also be paid.

Pensions

Controlling directors can obtain, along with other employees, pension benefits provided by the company. This means that pension schemes can be used as a method of applying company profits in a tax efficient manner for the benefit of working shareholders. Profits may be paid gross into a pension scheme where they will accumulate free of any tax liabilities and may be used to provide, within limits, tax free cash sums for a retiring director.

In view of the tax efficiency of these arrangements, the Inland Revenue place limits on the benefits which may be drawn from a pension scheme. These are generally related both to the length of time the individual has worked for the company and to the remuneration he has drawn from it. The principal limits are:

- an index-linked pension at retirement of up to two-thirds of the director's final remuneration provided he has worked for the employer for at least 10 years;
- part or all of the pension may be commuted for a tax free cash sum of up to one and a half times his final remuneration provided he has worked for the employer for at least 20 years;
- tax free life assurance cover of up to four times remuneration may be paid on death before retirement;

- a widow's pension of up to two-thirds of the member's own pension can be paid on death.

Each of these limits applies to 'final remuneration' and this can often be adjusted to provide optimum results for the director. For example, it is possible for directors to invest a substantial amount via pension contributions during their working lives and then, in the last three years before retirement, instead take substantially increased salaries. This will maximise the amount of tax free cash and pension they can draw from the scheme at retirement.

Since the limitations are expressed in terms of the benefits which may be drawn at retirement, there is no strict limit on the amount which may be paid into the scheme during the working life of the individual. However, the Inland Revenue will not allow the scheme to become 'over funded', ie more paid into the scheme than is required to provide the maximum benefits. Legislation in the Finance Act 1986 enforces this.

Remuneration:
Remuneration is widely defined and is not limited to basic salary. Bonuses, commissions and the taxable value of benefits in kind may also be included. However, since these can fluctuate from year to year, it is necessary to average them over three or more years.

Small self-administered schemes:
Rather than paying large pension contributions to insurance companies, a small self-administered pension scheme may be established which is, effectively, an exempt trust fund of which the directors are the trustees. As such, they control the investments of the fund and have power to invest almost anywhere. The Inland Revenue will wish to see that the investments are appropriate for the scheme (and that tax avoidance is not in point) but, subject to that, the directors retain control. For example, loans can be made back to the employing company at a commercial rate of interest or the employer's premises may be purchased by the pension fund and let to the company. The fund might also buy shares in the employing company.

Increasing remuneration:
In view of the tax efficiency of pension arrangements, it used to be appropriate for a controlling director to be granted a salary increase of 17.64%. This enabled him to make personal contributions of 15% of his revised remuneration. In this way, his taxable income remained unchanged but the maximum benefit which he could

draw from the pension scheme at retirement would be increased by 17.64%. This enabled him to make personal contributions of 15% of his revised remuneration. In this way, his taxable income remained unchanged but the maximum benefit which he could draw from the pension scheme at retirement would be increased by 17.64%. This can still be worthwhile, but the national insurance effect should be considered.

Investment company pensions:
In certain circumstances it is possible to establish a pension scheme for directors of an investment company. The maximum benefits which may be drawn on retirement are much lower than those which apply to a trading company unless the director has worked for the company for at least 40 years. Further, if part of the director's remuneration is disallowed in the company's tax computation, then benefits may be provided only in respect of the allowable sum.

Lloyd's agencies:
The requirement that contributions are normally relieved against income in the year in which they are paid is relaxed for companies in receipt of profit commission from Lloyd's. This is a concession and special rules apply. Furthermore, the concession applies to contributions paid by companies and the Inland Revenue is not prepared to extend it to individuals.

Employee benefits
Rather than paying employees additional remuneration, there can often be tax advantages in granting them benefits. For example:

Company cars:
It is usually reckoned that the tax charge accompanying the provision of the company car is less than the real benefit received.

Pensions:
Most employees value pension benefits provided that they are clearly explained to them. Many schemes, however, fail to impress employees simply because they are too difficult to understand or are badly explained. Properly used, however, a pension scheme can be a very attractive employee benefit which gives rise to no adverse tax charge for the employee.

Medical insurance:
Apart from being a worthwhile benefit in itself, company provision of medical insurance can also be highly cost effective since cover will

be available at cheaper rates than the employee could himself have obtained and, if an employee suffers an accident or illness, he will often be treated more quickly (and therefore return to work sooner) than if the cover had not been available.

Interest free loans:
Where an employee receives an interest free loan through his employment, he is taxed on the benefit. Tax is charged by assuming that his income is increased by the annual value of the loan, currently 12% pa. Similar rules apply to low interest loans.

However, no tax is charged if the employee uses the loan for a 'qualifying purpose' where he would obtain tax relief on the interest if he paid any. Consequently, an employer could lend money to an employee free of interest and no tax charge will result if the loan is used, for example, to purchase property in the UK which is let commercially. Alternatively, if the loan is used by the employee to purchase his main residence (not a second home), no tax charge will arise provided that the loan is less than £30,000.

In either case, the employee will acquire an asset which may be expected to grow in value, whilst his obligation to repay the loan will be fixed in money terms.

There will be no tax to pay where the annual value of the loan is under £200. This means that up to £1,660 might be lent to an employee for a year without any tax liability. Alternatively, if the annual value would be more than £200, it may be worthwhile the employee paying some interest in order to bring the net value to within the limit.

It should be borne in mind that loans to directors are regulated by the Companies Acts and can cause tax or legal problems.

Groups
Tax problems can arise, and tax benefits can be lost, where there are associated companies or there is a formal group structure.

Small companies rate:
Where a company has taxable profits of less than £100,000 it will suffer tax at a small companies rate of 29%. However, if there are any associated companies these limits are divided by the total number of companies so that, for example, if there were four associated companies, each would have to keep its profits within £25,000 to benefit from the small company rate.

Group structure:
There are different definitions of a 'group' for different tax

purposes. It is worthwhile reviewing a group to ensure that it is structured in the most appropriate way for tax purposes. Frequently, it is better to establish one company with different trading divisions rather than set up separate companies for different purposes.

Management charges:
Where management services are provided by one company to another an appropriate charge can be made. This will have the effect of moving taxable profits from one company to another, but it is essential that the level of the charge can be justified on purely commercial grounds.

VAT:
VAT in a group – particularly on management charges – should not be overlooked. This is a complex area and tax savings can often be made by reviewing the existing position with VAT specialists.

Avoiding apportionment
If a close company receives investment income, the Inland Revenue can, in some circumstances, apportion this among the shareholders. This may result in additional tax liabilities, but might be avoided by ensuring that investment income in the company is minimised by investing for capital growth.

Capital gains tax planning

Retirement relief
The provisions for obtaining relief from capital gains tax on retirement were substantially amended by the Finance Act 1985. From the planning point of view, there are several points to be borne in mind.

Age requirement:
Full relief from £100,000 of gain is now available from age 60 (or earlier if you have been forced to retire by ill health). It is not now necessary to work until 65 to obtain the full relief.

Ten year rule:
It is still necessary for you to have owned the business for ten years in order to obtain full relief.

Chargeable assets:
There is still a restriction on the amount of relief available if there are

capital gains within the business which are not entirely referable to
the business, eg on investments. Tax savings may be made by
reviewing the position in advance of the anticipated disposal of the
business.

Rent:
If you own a property which is let to the business, capital gains on
the property will not qualify for retirement relief to the extent to
which you have received a commercial rental. The position should
be reviewed in advance of the anticipated disposal since some tax
savings may be made by reducing or eliminating the rental
payments.

'Full-time':
In the case of a sale of company shares, it is necessary to show that
you have worked within the business full-time for a period of at least
ten years. Consequently, some relief might be lost if you
commenced working part time, although there are now provisions
allowing you to change to part time working in specific
circumstances.

Roll–over relief

A person who disposes of a business asset and reinvests the proceeds
in a new business asset may defer the charge to capital gains tax. The
old and the new asset need not be used in the same trade. Thus
someone selling business assets may reinvest, for example, in land to
be planted as commercial woodlands and thereby obtain long-term
CGT deferral.

Indexation

If you are purchasing an asset through the medium of a company
and borrowing capital to finance the purchase, there may be a choice
as to whether the capital should be borrowed by you personally or
by the company. If the company borrows and then repays the loans
out of profits, the amount of capital you have put into the company
(and therefore the base cost of your shares for CGT indexation
purposes) will be very low. On the other hand, if you borrow and
subscribe for a more valuable shareholding, indexation will be
available on a much higher sum.

The costs and methods of servicing the loan must, of course, be
considered, as must the imposition of additional capital duty on the
enlarged shareholding. Nevertheless, there can often be an
advantage in borrowing outside the company rather than within it.

Loans/guarantees

The Finance Act 1978 introduced a relief from capital gains tax where losses are incurred on loans or on guarantees for loans made to traders. The arrangement must have been effected after 11 April 1978 and it is therefore wise to review any existing loan or guarantees. It may be desirable to terminate and renew any in existence prior to 11 April 1978.

NIC planning

With the abolition of the upper earnings limit on employers' national insurance contributions, it is usually worthwhile reviewing the way in which employees are remunerated in order to minimise the burden of national insurance contributions.

Benefits

At present, NI contributions are payable on cash payments to an employee. Non-cash benefits such as provision of a car, medical insurance or pension rights do not attract NI contributions.

Care must be taken to avoid meeting an employee's liability, eg by settling a bill he has incurred. Whenever possible, the employer should contract directly with a third party to provide a benefit to the employee. This will not give rise to any income tax advantage (other than cash flow since the payments will attract tax via the employee's Form P11D rather than under PAYE) but NIC will be avoided.

Employee trusts

Where an employee receives a cash payment from a trust established by his employer, the payment is (at present) specifically exempted from national insurance contributions.

Pensions

Many pension schemes require employees to contribute towards them. Since an employee will have regard to this when reviewing his salary, it is arguable that, in reality, the employer ultimately bears the cost of this via a higher payroll. Consequently, contributory pension arrangements should be reconsidered, with a view to making them non–contributory.

Dividends

Shareholder directors should consider drawing dividends instead of additional remuneration. Although this will result in national insurance savings, there are a number of other factors which need to be taken into account which could outweigh these savings. These include the effect on share value, the impact on pension rights and the cash flow of the employer. The overall position should be considered carefully before any decisions are made.

Chapter 7
Planning for Members of Lloyd's

Becoming an underwriting member of Lloyd's involves using one's assets a second time to back an insurance business. There is substantial scope for financial planning and this section looks at the following areas:

- Proving means
- Providing the deposit
- Investment strategy
- Pensions
- Overseas members

Proving means

Means test

It is necessary to demonstrate to the Committee of Lloyd's that you have sufficient net wealth to meet potential claims. The assets must be freely marketable and have a recognised value. The value of your house is normally discounted and certain assets – works of art and private company shares – are generally ignored. However, although Lloyd's will not themselves accept these assets, they will accept a guarantee or letter of credit provided by an authorised bank which is secured on those assets. Needless to say, the bank will usually require substantial cover for the guarantee and so, for example, a guarantee secured on a painting might be limited to 35% of the painting's estimated value. Nevertheless, guarantees can be an extremely useful way of proving means where insufficient liquid capital is available.

Providing the deposit

Introduction

In order to commence underwriting, it is necessary to lodge a deposit with Lloyd's for 25% (35% for overseas members) of the premium income to be underwritten. Traditionally, stocks and shares have been lodged for this purpose, but it is increasingly popular to use a guarantee or letter of credit instead.

Lodging investments

Investments held in a deposit are registered in the name of Corporation of Lloyd's. Unless the whole of the deposit is in the form of UK Stock Exchange securities, Lloyd's require that at least 25% of the deposit is held in a safe form, cash or short dated gilts, for example. The remaining assets can be held in any liquid investment medium such as quoted equities.

Any income arising on the investments is paid out to the member. Capital growth is locked into the deposit and cannot be withdrawn except to meet a CGT liability. However, it may be used to increase underwriting commitments in the future and the growth will usually count as part of the individual's Lloyd's assets in calculating IHT business relief.

Guarantee

Assets may be pledged to a bank who then provide a guarantee or letter of credit to Lloyd's for the deposit. This can be more flexible since the bank may accept assets as collateral which could not themselves be put into the deposit, eg private company shares. Any capital growth could be used to increase the guarantee—and therefore the underwriting commitments—or could (by arrangement with the bank) be withdrawn for spending.

For inheritance tax purposes, provided the guarantee is properly secured on the underlying assets then business relief will be available on the underlying assets up to the face value of the guarantee.

As an alternative, guarantees can be obtained from an insurance company which can be very tax efficient in some circumstances. A lump sum is invested with the insurance company which is funded over a ten year period into an investment orientated policy which can provide tax free benefits after ten years. This has a number of advantages:

- The tax free benefits after ten years (including the facility for a tax free income) make this extremely attractive to higher rate taxpayers;
- The company provides a guarantee for the full amount of the cash lodged with it rather than requiring cover in excess of this amount;
- The insurance companies make no charge for the guarantee whereas a bank would usually charge 1% to 2% per annum.

In summary, a guarantee can be more flexible but lodging assets could give rise to greater inheritance tax benefits.

Investment strategy

'Bond washing'

Most Lloyd's members are higher rate tax payers and their investment strategy will be similar to that of other higher rate tax payers. In the past the profits from Lloyd's have often contained large elements of capital appreciation but this may well change following the introduction of new rules on 'bond washing' in the Finance Act 1985. This may have the effect of substantially increasing syndicate investment income and so the following points should be borne in mind:

Growth

If syndicate investment income does increase, this will add to the member's taxable income and make it more important that personal investments are orientated more for growth than for income. For example, gilts and cash deposits might be switched into the very low coupon index linked gilts.

SRF transfers

The increase in syndicate investment income may allow larger amounts to be transferred into the special reserve fund although the overriding maximum of £7,000 gross still applies.

Business Expansion Scheme

The Business Expansion Scheme allows capital investments of up to £40,000 per annum to be written off against income for tax purposes. Consequently, tax on additional income might be deferred or avoided by investment through the BES. However, bear in mind that BES shares cannot be included as assets for means test purposes.

Inheritance tax planning

Introduction

Underwriting at Lloyd's constitutes a business for IHT business relief purposes. Consequently, the assets used in the business – the deposit, reserves (within reason) and open years of account – all qualify for a 50% tax relief for IHT purposes. However, this tax relief is wasted if the member's will leaves the business to his wife (which transfer is exempt from tax) and she does not qualify for the relief when she passes the assets on unless she herself becomes an underwriting member.

It makes sense to ensure that Lloyd's assets do not pass to a surviving spouse but instead are left to other beneficiaries or to a flexible trust fund. For example, the assets could pass into a discretionary trust under which income and capital can be paid to a widow during her lifetime but where the underlying assets do not form part of her estate for tax purposes.

Reserves

Since assets held in a personal or special reserve fund constitute Lloyd's assets qualifying for business relief (providing they are not excessive relative to the level of underwriting) it can be beneficial to increase reserve funds and thereby increase the potential tax relief.

Pensions

Personal pension plan

Where an underwriter has Working Name status he may pay contributions to a personal pension plan in respect of his underwriting profits. Contributions in respect of any 1983 Account profits must be paid prior to 5 April 1987. Earnings are calculated after any special reserve fund transfer, guarantee charges, etc.

Overseas members

Because underwriting at Lloyd's constitutes a business in the UK, income associated with it is taxable in the UK.

Minimising UK income

From 1987, an overseas member will be permitted to provide the deposit by way of acceptable UK securities and/or sterling to be held in the Lloyd's Group Account Scheme. In every case, a power of attorney must be given in the UK with authority to make investment decisions on the member's behalf. However, such investment will give rise to UK taxable income and therefore will not generally be attractive. Alternatively an overseas member may fund his deposit by a bank guarantee. The assets backing the guarantee should not be invested to give rise to UK taxable income and so should either be invested offshore or in exempt gilt stocks in the UK.

Many underwriting agents require members to establish a personal reserve to be used for solvency purposes and for the funding of underwriting losses. Rather than holding investments in the reserves, a guarantee can again be used.

Foreign tax credit restriction

A member resident in any overseas territory where he pays local tax on Lloyd's income may be in a position where his average rate of tax in the UK is higher than in his home country. This may result in a limitation being applied to the credit against his home country tax which he can obtain for the UK tax paid. One way around this is to invest his Lloyd's assets in such a way that no additional UK tax is incurred, but the level of Lloyd's income is increased, so that the average rate of tax falls.

Chapter 8

Planning with Trusts

Trusts can be established for a very wide range of reasons. This section looks at trusts under the following headings:

- Introduction
- Types of trust
- Practical points

Introduction

What is a trust?

A trust separates the legal ownership of an asset from the beneficial ownership (or the enjoyment) of the asset. Trustees legally own the assets, but the beneficiaries will benefit from them. This has taxation implications and establishing trusts will often result in a substantial tax saving. The settlor is the person who creates the trust and transfers assets into it.

Objectives

Apart from setting up trusts to obtain tax advantages, trusts also enable a person to achieve objectives which would otherwise not be possible. For example, children cannot deal with assets for themselves. Others are unable to manage assets for themselves even when they reach the age of majority. In these situations trusts can hold assets on their behalf.

Trusts can be used to achieve purely personal objectives, for example where a man wishes to allow his widow to use his assets during her lifetime but wants to ensure that they pass to pre-determined beneficiaries on her death rather than being distributed in accordance with her will.

Trustee duties

The trustees are charged with the responsibility of running the trust fund in accordance with the terms set out in the trust deed and in accordance with general legal principles. They are required to act impartially and to consider the position of all of the beneficiaries. They must not use the fund to benefit themselves as trustees.

Beneficiaries

These people ultimately benefit from the trust. They may be named individually in the trust deed or may be members of a class, eg children or grandchildren of the settlor.

Beneficiaries may also be trustees of the fund, although in such cases they must remember that they are legally two different people and must remember in which capacity they are acting.

Time limits

UK trusts cannot continue indefinitely (unless they are purely charitable) but must come to an end after a period of time. In most cases the maximum life of a trust will be 80 years, although it can be longer. During the first 21 years of a trust the law may allow the trustees to accumulate any income instead of paying it out. After 21 years, in most cases, income must be distributed among the beneficiaries.

Types of trust

There are different types of trust for tax purposes as follows:

Discretionary trusts

When a discretionary trust is set up, the trustees will have discretion as to who is to benefit from the trust assets. Appropriate trust powers may enable income to be paid out or accumulated and trust capital may be advanced to any of the beneficiaries. None of the beneficiaries have any pre-determined rights to claim the income arising and normally they will have no right to the capital either. Instead, the trustees are given complete discretion as to which of the beneficiaries will receive either capital or income and at what stage.

In this way, discretionary trusts enable assets to be held in suspense for a wide class of beneficiaries, some of whom may not yet be born. Different beneficiaries may receive benefits from the fund but for tax purposes the fund is not treated as belonging to any of them. The tax position is as follows:

Income tax:
If the settlor can benefit from the fund in any way, then the whole of the income arising within the fund (if any) will be taxed as if it were his income, whether he receives it or not. From the income tax point of view, therefore, the settlor can be in exactly the same position as if he had not transferred the investment to the trust.

If the settlor cannot benefit under the fund (or after the settlor's death) any income which is accumulated will suffer tax at 45%.

Income which is paid out will be taxed in the beneficiary's hands at his own rate. This can be very useful as a way of using minor children's tax allowances where life policies have matured on their father's death.

Inheritance tax:
Since the assets are held in suspense and cannot be taxed as belonging to any of the beneficiaries, a special regime has been introduced to tax the assets held in a discretionary trust. They suffer a charge once every ten years, with a top-up charge on any capital distributed in the interim. Tax is calculated at 30% of the lifetime IHT rates and this means that the absolute maximum charge (ie for very large trusts) is 9% of the value of the fund, once every ten years. Although this is, in itself, a small price to pay for the ultimate flexibility of a discretionary trust, the actual charge is usually very much lower and can often be nil if the value of the fund is kept within the nil rate band of IHT (currently £71,000). Consequently, rather than establish one large trust, it is usually beneficial to establish a series of smaller separate trusts. Provided that each trust commences on a different day they will not be related for IHT purposes.

Where the settlor is included as a beneficiary under a trust set up after 17 March 1986, it seems that this will be regarded as a 'gift with reservation' and the property in the trust will still be taxed as part of his estate.

Capital gains tax:
Trusts have the benefit of an annual CGT exemption of up to £3,150. However, where one settlor has made a number of settlements (other than non resident or charitable trusts, or trusts for the mentally disabled) after 6 June 1978, the £3,150 exemption is divided by the number of such settlements, subject to a minimum exemption of £630 per settlement. Trustees should consider realising gains each year to utilise the exemption.

Using discretionary trusts
Because discretionary trusts are so flexible they can be used in almost any situation:

Uncertainty:
A settlor can keep his options open in terms of who can benefit from the fund and at what stage. This is often important where the prospective beneficiaries are very young.

Holding vehicles: A discretionary trust is ideal for holding cash and investments where income and capital are to be paid to different beneficiaries at different times, eg for providing for a widow and children.

Retaining control:
The settlor can himself be a trustee. The underlying capital will not, however, be taxed as part of his estate provided that he has no entitlement to benefit. The position following the Finance Act 1986 appears to be that where a benefit is retained the initial settlement will be regarded as a gift with reservation.

Restructuring:
Most discretionary trusts are sufficiently flexible to be restructured into, perhaps, an interest in possession or accumulation and maintenance trust if that were to become more appropriate in the future.

Interest in possession trusts

An interest in possession trust arises where a beneficiary has a *right* to claim the income of the trust fund or to use the property comprised in it. Quite often, the beneficiary having this right will be different from the person or persons who may ultimately inherit the capital. Alternatively, it may be provided that the beneficiary may have the income until he attains the age of 21 or 25 years perhaps, when he will also receive the capital.

An interest in possession can exist even where there is no income arising so that the beneficiary actually receives nothing, eg where private company shares are not paying a dividend. The important factor is that the beneficiary should be able to claim the income if there is any.

Income tax:
The income arising is taxed as the beneficiary's.

Inheritance tax:
The capital underlying the beneficiary's interest in possession is deemed to belong to the beneficiary himself and so it will be taxed as a gift on his death or if his interest ceases during his lifetime, for example if he gives it away. However, if the capital passes back to the settlor (or to the settlor's wife not later than two years after his death) the gift will be exempt from tax. For trusts established after 17 March 1986, if the settlor is included as a possible beneficiary, the assets in the trust may be regarded as still forming part of his estate.

Capital gains tax:
As for a discretionary trust, above.

Using interest in possession trusts
These are most useful where there are one or more ascertained beneficiaries and it is known what benefits are to be provided for them.

Will trusts:
A husband may wish to leave his estate so that his widow can continue to live in the home and receive the income from his investments, etc, but ensure that the underlying capital passes to pre-determined beneficiaries on her death. This may be particularly important where the parties have previous marriages.

Spendthrifts:
Where there is fear that the beneficiaries may spend the underlying capital, their interest may be restricted to the income so that the capital is preserved.

Life policies:
Interest in possession settlements are particularly useful where life policies are involved. This is because a policy does not produce any income until after it has matured and the proceeds have been invested elsewhere. Consequently, a beneficiary having an interest in possession where the underlying asset is a life policy will receive nothing during the lifetime of the life assured. When the proceeds are eventually received by the trustees they might either invest them (paying the income to the beneficiary) or might pay the underlying capital out either to the 'primary' beneficiary or to any other beneficiary who might benefit under the trust.

Accumulation and maintenance trusts
These are trusts for the benefit of a class of minor children and can be very useful where an individual wishes to provide for his children or grandchildren. This type of trust can include both existing and unborn beneficiaries (within certain limits) and so are very flexible. Income can be paid out for the 'maintenance, education or advancement' of the beneficiaries and any income not paid out must be accumulated within the trust.

In order to attract important IHT concessions, the trust must provide for at least one of the beneficiaries to become entitled to at least an interest in possession (see above) in the fund not later than the age of 25. However, any entitlement to the underlying capital itself can be deferred for a prolonged period.

Income tax:
Any income accumulated will be taxed at 45%.

Income paid out to a beneficiary will be taxed in his hands, unless the beneficiary is a minor child of the settlor in which case the income will be taxed at the settlor's top rate.

Alternatively, where it is desired to avoid both the 45% tax rate within the trust and the possibility of aggregation with the parent's income, income can be advanced into a separate bare trust for the child's benefit.

Inheritance tax:
Although none of the beneficiaries have any fixed entitlements until they attain, perhaps, the age of 25, there is no ten yearly charge (as with an ordinary discretionary trust) and there is no tax charge when beneficiaries receive their interest. In most circumstances, an accumulation and maintenance trust will attract no inheritance tax liability, with the original settlement being a potentially exempt transfer.

Capital gains tax:
As for a discretionary trust, above.

Using accumulation and maintenance trusts
These are most appropriate where there are one or two young children in a family and the settlor wishes to make provision for them and their future brothers and sisters.

School fees:
Where the capital is given by someone other than the parent (eg a grandparent) then the income arising can be paid out to the child or for his benefit and will be tax free within his personal allowance. This is a good way of funding school fee liabilities.

Generation skipping:
Where children are already well provided for, it is often advantageous for grandparents to pass assets to grandchildren, thereby skipping one generation and avoiding one layer of IHT charges. Accumulation and maintenance trusts provide an ideal vehicle for this.

Bare trusts
Assets are held on bare trusts where both capital and income are

held by the trustees for a named and living individual and no conditions remain to be fulfilled before the individual can claim the trust funds. Gifts made to minors will usually be held by the parents on bare trust until the child reaches age 18.

Income tax:
Income arising belongs to the beneficiary and will be taxed as part of his income. However, income arising on gifts made by a child's parents will usually be treated as the parent's income unless that income is accumulated under the terms of the trust and not paid or applied for the benefit of the child. Accumulating income in these circumstances can be tax free up to the child's personal allowance of £2,335.

Inheritance tax:
The underlying capital belongs to the beneficiary and will be taxed as part of his estate in the usual way.

Capital gains tax:
The capital belongs to the beneficiary and any capital gains arising will be taxed in his hands.

Using bare trusts
From the tax planning point of view, these are appropriate where income from a disposition by a minor child's parent is to be accumulated to avoid aggregation with the parent's income for tax purposes.

Charitable trusts
Charitable trusts arise where funds are held for the exclusive benefit of charitable objects. All income arising in a fund must be used for charitable purposes only. Charitable trusts may continue indefinitely.

Charitable trusts are usually exempt from income tax, inheritance tax and capital gains tax. Provisions of the Finance Act 1986 may restrict tax exemptions in certain situations.

Using charitable trusts
These are an ideal vehicle if you wish to benefit different charities in a tax-efficient way, but do not want to commit yourself to continue supporting any one charity. Capital can be transferred into the trust (free of CGT and IHT) or income may be covenanted to the charitable trust, attracting full income tax relief. This relief may be restricted if the requirements of the Finance Act 1986 are not met.

Income and capital within the trust can then be distributed for any charitable purpose by the trustees (who usually include the donor). Where small amounts are involved, it can be more cost effective to use a body like the Charities Aid Foundation, rather than establish your own personal charitable trust.

Pilot trusts

These are simply trusts which are created in advance of the time when they are expected to be used. They usually hold a nominal sum, perhaps £25, and are established as a holding vehicle so that property can be added in the future, eg pension scheme death benefits. Pilot trusts are usually discretionary, but might have an interest in possession or might qualify as accumulation and maintenance trusts.

Overseas trusts

Most trusts are established in the UK with UK resident trustees. Sometimes, however, it may be advantageous for a trust (usually either a discretionary trust or an interest in possession trust) to be resident overseas in order to defer, or perhaps avoid, capital gains tax liabilities. For CGT purposes, the residence of a trust is determined by the residence of the majority of the trustees and the place of administration. The trust will usually suffer tax on income and capital gains arising according to the tax laws of the country of residence.

Generally, there is no income tax advantage in establishing a trust overseas unless the settlor or the beneficiaries are not resident or not domiciled in the UK. However, there can be a capital gains tax advantage since CGT may not be payable on capital gains made by the trustees until capital is advanced to a UK resident beneficiary. The liability can therefore be deferred and, if beneficiaries are neither resident nor ordinarily resident in the UK when capital is paid to them, tax may be avoided completely.

From the IHT point of view, overseas trusts can be extremely tax efficient where the settlor is not domiciled in the UK, but there is no IHT advantage where the settlor is domiciled in the UK.

Practical points

After a trust has been established, taxation and administrative advantages can often be obtained by regularly reviewing the situation.

Investments

Investments may be made in a very wide range of areas for either capital growth or income production. The investments can be chosen to coincide with the needs of the beneficiaries of the trust. There can often be an administrative advantage in changing the investments. For example, a portfolio of stocks and shares gives rise to substantial paper work in terms of dividends, scrip issues, rights issues, takeovers etc. There is also the practical problem of managing the investments. Many of these problems can be eliminated by investing in unit trusts where the day to day administration and investment management is dealt with by professionals.

Where there is no requirement for an income to be produced, there may be merit in investing the trust fund into a non-income producing asset such as National Savings Certificates (providing a guaranteed tax free return) or investment bonds. See Part 3.

Winding up

It is sometimes found that trusts continue in existence after they have outlived their original purpose. Alternatively, tax laws may have changed in the interim making the present structure inappropriate. In either case, a trust might be wound up or amended, thereby saving considerable expense. In a straightforward case, the trustees may have power to determine the trust or all of the beneficiaries may resolve to bring it to an end. In some cases, an application to the Court may be required.

Chapter 9

Planning for Expatriates

This chapter considers the planning opportunities open to:

- UK individuals going abroad
- UK individuals living abroad
- overseas individuals coming to and living in the UK

UK individuals going abroad

In all of the organisation required in preparing to live or work overseas some of the financial and taxation consequences can easily be overlooked. Yet there are a number of tax traps for the unwary and there are a number of opportunities which can be taken.

Double tax agreements

You should review your prospective tax position in your new country, together with any double taxation agreement between the UK and that country. By careful planning, it may be that particular items of income or capital gain may be taxed in neither country. In particular, bear in mind that the UK tax year runs from 6 April to 5 April whereas most other countries work on a calendar year basis. There may be merit in timing your arrival to be early in the new year rather than late in the old year.

Defer capital gains

You will be liable to UK capital gains tax on any gains made whilst you are either resident or ordinarily resident in the UK. If you are going abroad for a prolonged period, you should defer realising capital gains until after the date of your departure. If you are selling a business, you should ensure that the contract is not made until after you have left.

Defer income

Tax may also be saved if you defer income from arising until after you have left the UK. This might include rearranging investments, bank deposits, etc so that interest and dividends arise after the date of your departure. Regard must be had, however, to any double tax agreements.

Likewise, there may be an advantage in deferring realisation of any gains from off-shore money funds, etc.

Clean break

It is usually advantageous to ensure that you make a clean break from the UK for tax purposes. This may involve disposing of any accommodation you have available for your use in the UK or deferring any visits to the UK.

Wife

Although a couple may go to live abroad, often the wife will continue to be treated as UK resident. This might be advantageous if she has little income in her own name, but she might claim UK tax relief, eg on life assurance premiums.

UK individuals living abroad

Many UK individuals living overseas – particularly those in the traditional tax havens – may consider themselves to be completely outside the UK tax net. This is not always the case but, despite the problems, there are many opportunities open to those living abroad.

Double tax agreement

If there is a double tax agreement between the UK and your host country, this should be reviewed carefully since it will override the domestic law in both countries.

Beware UK residence

Unless you are working full-time overseas (and not in the UK) then you may continue to be treated as a UK resident if you set foot in the UK in any year in which you have accommodation available for your use. Thus you might inadvertently acquire UK residence (and thereby become liable to UK tax on your worldwide income) if you acquire a property in the UK.

This is particularly relevant where a wife is living with her husband abroad, but is not in full time employment. Often, she will continue to be treated as resident in the UK and therefore liable to tax on her worldwide income.

These problems can often be overcome by using the double tax agreement, if one exists.

Investment

Investment in the UK is usually avoided, since income arising in the UK is normally liable to UK tax. However, this may be overridden by a double tax agreement which might provide for a reduced rate of UK tax or even complete exemption. In these circumstances, relief should be claimed.

Pensions

Although pensions arising in the UK are normally liable to UK tax, special relief or exemption may be available under the double tax agreement and this should be claimed.

Domicile

If you are endeavouring to demonstrate that you are not domiciled in the UK but have taken up a domicile of choice in your new country, then it is important to minimise any links with the UK. For example, regular prolonged return visits could be fatal to a claim for non-domiciled status.

If you consider that you have already acquired non-domiciled status, you might consider transferring your capital to a trust as an insurance against the possibility of either yourself or your wife returning to the UK and your UK domicile reviving.

If you have had a UK domicile, you should remember that you can be deemed to continue to have a UK domicile for up to *four* years from the date of your departure from the UK.

MIRAS

If you pay mortgage interest on a property in the UK, you may be eligible to claim tax relief on the interest paid under the MIRAS system, even through you are not otherwise liable to tax here.

Returning

If you are returning to the UK, it is essential that you review your entire financial and tax position well in advance of returning. Failure to do so could result in UK tax becoming payable on income and capital gains which have actually been earned during your period abroad.

Overseas individuals coming to and living in the UK

Although the UK is normally considered to be a high tax country, it can be a tax haven for non-domiciled individuals who carefully arrange their financial affairs.

Double tax agreement

It is essential that any double tax agreement is carefully reviewed since this overrides any domestic law. For example, it may result in your continuing to be taxed as if you resided in your home country rather than in the UK.

Remittances

Income

You will become liable for UK tax on any income arising within the UK and on any income remitted to the UK from overseas. No income tax can be charged if you remit capital. It is essential therefore to segregate overseas income and capital into separate accounts so that it can be demonstrated clearly to the UK authorities that remittances are from capital rather than a mixed account. These rules do not apply to citizens of the Republic of Ireland who are resident in the UK: they are liable to UK tax on their worldwide income, whether remitted or not.

It may also be advantageous to open separate accounts to receive the income from individual investments if these are likely to be sold in the future. It may then be possible to remit the accumulated income from those investments after they have been realised.

There are 'constructive remittance' rules which can apply if the income accumulated overseas is used for your benefit in the UK.

Capital gains

Likewise, capital gains are liable to UK tax to the extent to which they are remitted (or constructively remitted) to the UK. If you remit a part of the proceeds, the Revenue will argue that that part includes a proportion of the capital gain. So hold the proceeds of any assets sold at a profit in an account separate from the 'pure' capital account.

Foreign earnings

If you continue to perform work overseas for an overseas employer, then your earnings from that work will be assessable in the UK to the extent that they are remitted or constructively remitted.

Inheritance tax

Any assets which you own in the UK will be liable to IHT. Consequently, you should avoid holding valuable assets in the UK in your own name. If you do wish to have large resources in the UK – properties or a company, for example – it is usually advantageous to hold these via an off-shore company. However, this is not always an ideal solution for a house in the UK.

If you continue to live in the UK on a prolonged basis, you may become regarded as domiciled in the UK and this would result in your worldwide assets becoming liable to UK inheritance tax. This might be avoided by transferring those assets into an off-shore trust before you become UK domiciled.

PART 3
INVESTMENTS

Chapter 10
Alternative Investments

Energy and films
A number of arrangements for direct investment in oil and gas exploration and development are available. There are also schemes marketed for investment in film production, particularly British films. The merits of these frequently hinge on commercial considerations although some involve taxation advantages. The tax consequences depend on the exact nature of the specific arrangements and require detailed consideration.

Commodities
The potential for high reward is the reason many investors are attracted to commodities. The potential for losses is equally great. The basic transactions in commodities are of three types:

- Physical or 'spot' transactions
- Futures
- Options

Commodities can be categorised broadly into 'metals' and 'softs' such as sugar and cocoa. Soft prices are much more volatile than metal prices, being particularly susceptible to weather conditions and crop failures. Professional advice and management is essential and a large element of risk needs to be accepted.

There is no clearly defined statutory method for taxing commodity transactions. The approach of the Inland Revenue may well be influenced by whether a profit has been made or a loss incurred.

Antiques and works of art
Antiques and works of art are more often than not purchased for aesthetic reasons and more in the hope that they will appreciate in value rather than as a pure investment. A collector may well be able to realise significant profits from a particular painting or collection if sold at auction. Works of art can be used by members of Lloyd's to support a guarantee for their Lloyd's deposit. If the particular works of art are of national, scientific, or historical interest, it may be possible to claim relief from IHT in respect of them.

Professional advice will almost certainly be required before any funds are committed. The taxation implications will vary depending upon the nature and type of transaction involved.

Advantages
Long-term rewards. Aesthetic qualities (works of art).

Disadvantages
High risk. Produce little or no income. Costs.

Ideal use
Wealthy individuals. Collectors (works of art).

Taxation treatment
Uncertain tax treatment. Losses may not be allowed.

Chapter 11
AVCs

Introduction

Additional voluntary contributions can often be made to an employer's pension scheme, and these can be extremely attractive from both the investment and taxation points of view if you wish to save for retirement. The contributions are deducted from your salary so that you receive full income tax relief on each payment, and are invested in a fund which suffers no tax. Consequently your savings will grow in value at a much faster rate than if you invest personally. However, the plan cannot be cashed in until you retire, at which time part (or all) may be drawn in cash, with any balance providing a pension.

Taxation

Full income tax relief can be obtained if you make regular payments over, normally, five or more years. The maximum amount you can invest is 15% of your earnings, less any contributions you are already making to your employer's pension scheme.

Your contributions will be invested in a fund which will not normally suffer any income tax, capital gains tax or corporation tax. If investment income is received by the fund net of tax – eg dividends – the tax deducted can usually be reclaimed.

At retirement, you are entitled to draw a tax free lump sum from the pension scheme as a whole, and often this means that your AVC fund can be encashed and drawn out tax free. However, the exact amount you are allowed to draw out will depend on how long you have worked for the employer and on your earnings. Also, if the basic pension scheme already gives you a cash sum, this must be taken into account.

Investment

The AVCs can be invested in a number of ways. Usually, they accumulate in a separate account in your own name, rather than being pooled with the general funds.

The most popular investment vehicles are:

- Building societies, where the contributions accumulate in an

ordinary building society account, but with a tax free rate of interest, currently around 10.75% pa.
- Life company pension policies, where contributions can buy units in a fund or group of funds, or can purchase guaranteed benefits to which bonuses are added – see Chapter 28 on Life Assurance.

Advantages
Tax relief on investments and tax free accumulation.

Disadvantages
Fund locked up until retirement.

Ideal use
Saving for retirement.

Taxation treatment
Tax relief on contributions. Tax free fund build-up. Possible tax free encashment at retirement.

Chapter 12
Bank Deposits

Introduction
Some banks pay interest on current accounts and there is now a wide range of interest bearing accounts available from both UK and overseas banks, here in the UK and offshore (eg Isle of Man, Channel Islands).

High interest accounts
The standard bank deposit account pays a relatively low rate of interest, but withdrawals can be made at any time and of any amount. Higher rates of interest are available for larger sums, eg £10,000+, if placed on either fixed-term or fixed notice deposit. In addition there are various money market or group deposit accounts where some of the highest rates may be obtained.

There are now available cheque book deposit accounts. These are offered by both merchant banks and clearing banks and pay high rates of interest provided the balance on the account does not fall below a certain level, eg £2,000. The rates of interest are published in the financial press. Additions and withdrawals by cheque can be made at any time in almost any amount. There is usually no charge for the provision of the cheque book but there may be a minimum amount for each cheque, eg £250. The rates of interest can vary considerably.

Taxation
Because of the introduction of the composite rate scheme of tax deduction at source it is not possible to receive gross interest, except in certain special circumstances (a deposit of over £50,000 for a period of 28 days or more). The tax deducted at source is not recoverable by non-taxpayers who might consider instead the National Savings Investment Account. Alternatively, there are non-UK branches (Channel Islands) of UK banks offering a full banking service but who are outside the scope of the composite rate scheme and who can pay interest gross.

See also

●   Building Society Accounts

Advantages
Wide choice of accounts. Cheque book facilities.

Disadvantages
No capital appreciation. Tendency to keep balances too high.

Ideal use
Short-term investments. Low risk.

Taxation treatment
Composite rate tax not recoverable.

Chapter 13

Building Society Accounts

Introduction
Building societies provide a relatively safe and simple method of savings and investment. This goes some way to explaining their popularity. The range and variety of accounts now on offer are such that it pays to 'shop around'. The amount of your investment, whether you need immediate access to the funds and whether you are prepared to accept interest penalties will dictate the most appropriate account. It is often possible to increase the rate of interest payable by as much as 2% simply by switching to another account with the same society. It is among the smaller building societies, which do not have an extensive branch network, that some of the most competitive accounts can be found.

Guarantees
Some building societies offer guarantees. It is essential to check just what is guaranteed: usually it is the differential over the ordinary share account rate. If the ordinary share rate drops, in line with market rates of interest, then the rate paid on the guaranteed account will also fall. Few building societies offer a guaranteed rate of interest, but one or two regularly offer one, two or three year guaranteed bonds.

Cheque books
A new departure is the building society account with a cheque book facility. These are a direct response to the cheque book deposit accounts marketed by some banks. It is necessary to compare the rates on offer to see if an account with a building society or a bank offers the better value for money.

Taxation
Tax is deducted at source from building society interest and is not reclaimable except on certain accounts opened by non-residents or pension funds. A building society account may not be the most appropriate for non-taxpayers, particularly if a higher gross return is available.

See also
- Bank Deposits

Advantages
Simple. Branch network. Passbook. Easy access.

Disadvantages
No capital appreciation. Interest not guaranteed.

Ideal use
Low risk short term funds.

Taxation treatment
Usually no repayment of tax deducted at source.

Chapter 14
Bulldog Bonds

Description
These are securities issued in the UK by foreign governments or corporations and denominated in sterling. Higher yields are generally available than on gilts but they are less marketable and carry a greater element of risk. The CGT treatment mirrors that for gilts.

Advantages
High gross return.

Disadvantages
Not so freely marketable as gilts. Not as secure as gilts.

Ideal use
Securing high fixed income for fixed period.

Taxation treatment
Interest taxable and paid net. Capital gains can be tax free.

Chapter 15

Business Expansion Scheme

Introduction

The BES was introduced by the Finance Act 1983 and was originally due to end on 5 April 1987. However, the Finance Act 1986 has extended its life indefinitely. Under the scheme you are able to obtain income tax relief when subscribing for eligible shares in certain unquoted companies. There are complex rules defining the companies and types of business which qualify. The rules also determine the type of shares which may be issued and whether or not you as a subscriber can claim relief.

The maximum allowable investment in any tax year is £40,000 and this limit applies to the joint investment of a married couple. There have been changes made to the BES rules since the scheme began, and the most important current restriction excludes most companies with 50% of their net assets in the form of land and buildings.

Approved funds

Approved funds act like unit trusts and channel investors' money into unquoted companies. There are risks involved in an investment in unquoted companies. The approved funds employ professional managers to make investment decisions and to place their investments. They also spread the risk over many companies. The funds usually levy charges to both the investor and the company and will often take options to subscribe for shares at a fixed price at a later date.

Taxation

The BES shares must be held for at least five years to retain the income tax relief, otherwise there may be a clawback. The Finance Act 1986 introduced an exemption from CGT on the gain arising on a disposal of the shares after five years where those shares were originally acquired after 18 March 1986. The company itself must satisfy the qualifying conditions for at least three years in order to preserve the relief.

If you, as a BES investor, can acquire at least 5% of the company then it may be possible to borrow the funds required for the investment and claim tax relief on the borrowing.

Advantages
Medium-term growth prospects. Approved funds.

Disadvantages
High risk. Charges. Complex tax rules.

Ideal use
Higher rate taxpayers.

Taxation treatment
Income tax relief. CGT exemption.

Chapter 16

Capital Conversion Plans

Introduction
Capital conversion plans – sometimes called back-to-back arrangements – use Maximum Investment Plans (see Chapter 30) but, instead of the premiums being met out of income, a lump sum of capital is set aside at the beginning to provide for future premiums. The capital must be deployed in a way which will fund the premiums with the minimum of administration and in both a cost effective and tax efficient way. The arrangement can also provide income over the ten year period, if required.

Funding methods
There are several methods of funding available:

- direct transfers from capital, realising a lump sum each year to pay the annual premiums;
- purchase of a temporary annuity to provide for the next nine premiums, the first premium to be provided out of available capital;
- guaranteed insurance bonds maturing each year to provide a series of annual sums to pay premiums;
- a basket of gilt stocks designed to mature or be sold each year with the capital and accumulated income being used to pay premiums.

This is not an exhaustive list and the merits of any one method depend upon the particular circumstances. Care must be taken, if the MIP is to be written upon trust, to ensure that the entire capital sum is not treated as a gift and perhaps chargeable to IHT.

Lloyd's members
Certain types of capital conversion plan are available to members of Lloyd's to enable them to provide their deposit. These involve the issue of a guarantee and advice should be sought before a commitment is made (see Chapter 7).

IHT planning
Capital conversion plans can be an efficient way of mitigating IHT

liabilities. The MIP can be arranged under a trust to mature IHT free whilst a funding annuity will not be taxed in the investor's estate.

Chapter 17
Discounted Gift Plans

Discounted gift and income plans

A number of CTT planning arrangements were until recently available based on two types of life assurance contract, a pure endowment single premium investment bond and a term assurance policy (the term PETA was often used to describe them). Under the arrangement, capital invested passed free of CTT on your death whilst you could retain an income during your lifetime. The term assurance policy was arranged under a trust.

Taxation

For CTT purposes, the investment was treated as a gift at the time it was made. However, as the capital did not pass to the intended beneficiaries until your death it was discounted (based on a formula agreed with the Inland Revenue) in determining the value of the gift.

However, the 1986 Finance Act (which, as mentioned previously, replaces CTT with IHT) contains provisions relating to 'gifts with reservation', thought to have been introduced (in part) to counteract such schemes. Notwithstanding this, it may well be possible for life assurance companies to devise new schemes of similar effect.

Chapter 18

Enterprise Zones

Introduction
The construction or purchase unused of certain industrial, commercial or retail buildings in designated Enterprise Zones qualifies for capital allowances. The allowances include a 100% initial allowance, all or part of which can be disclaimed if it would be advantageous to do so. If any part of the initial allowance is disclaimed, an annual writing down allowance is due at the rate of 25% pa. In all situations, the total allowances due cannot exceed the total eligible expenditure on the building, not the land.

There are some 40 or so designated Enterprise Zones in different locations around the UK. As well as tax concessions the zones benefit from freedom of planning restrictions and a moratorium on rates.

Loans
Investment in industrial or commercial property, whether in an Enterprise Zone or outside, requires a large capital outlay. The proposed investment should be made on commercial grounds alone, with the tax concessions acting as a bonus. It is possible to gear up an investment by way of loans, secured on the property, the interest on which is deductible from the rental income derived from letting the building.

Example:	£
Cost of new unused building	100,000
Tax relief at, say, 60%	(60,000)
Actual cost	40,000
Loan	(40,000)
Cash outlay	NIL
Rental yield, say 7% pa	7,000
Loan interest payable, say	(5,600)
	1,400
Income tax at, say, 60%	(840)
Annual net income	560

In the above example if no action had been taken, tax at 60% would have been deducted from income of £100,000, leaving £40,000 spendable. The purchase of a building in an Enterprise Zone for £100,000, coupled with a loan of £40,000, leaves the same amount spendable but with the potential for capital appreciation on the building and the opportunity to increase future rental income by reviews.

Disposal
A disposal of a building on which capital allowances have been granted within 25 years usually gives rise to a charge to claw-back part or all of the tax relief given. However, the grant of a lease does not always count as a disposal and can therefore avoid this claw-back. A suitable lessee in this case might be a pension fund (perhaps a small self-adminstered scheme) which would receive the rental income tax free.

Advantages
Long-term capital appreciation. Ability to borrow (secured).

Disadvantages
Large capital outlay. Costs. Land law.

Ideal use
Higher rate taxpayers.

Taxation treatment
100% initial capital allowances. Loan interest qualifies for income tax relief.

Chapter 19
Equity Investment

Equities
All companies have a defined amount of issued equity capital, which is divided into shares of a particular nominal or 'par' value. A company could have £1 million issued share capital divided into 4 million ordinary 25p shares. What matters more than its par value is the market value of a share.

Valuation
The market value of an unquoted share (ie a share which is not dealt-in on a recognised Stock Exchange) is difficult to ascertain but tax liabilities are generally calculated by reference to market value, even where no market exists. The value of a share which is part of a majority (at least 51%) holding will be significantly greater than the value of a share in a minority holding. Shares in unquoted companies sometimes qualify under the Business Expansion Scheme, as business property for relief from IHT (50% or 30%) and for relief from income tax on losses.

Markets
Shares quoted on the Unlisted Securities Market (USM) or the full Stock Exchange are marketable and it is possible to obtain a price depending on whether you are buying or selling. Equity investment is risky but by spreading the risk over a number of shares in different sectors of the Stock Market it can be minimised. It is essential to use a stockbroker to buy or sell shares or to deal through an organisation which in turn deals with a stockbroker. When a new company comes to the market, or if there is a new issue of shares in an existing company, you can apply direct without using a broker.

The Over The Counter (OTC) market is not regulated by the Stock Exchange but by individual market makers. Some operate on a 'matched bargain' basis whilst others act as both jobber and stockbroker and actually fix the prices of the stocks in which they deal.

Dividends
The dividends from shares are paid subject to advance corporation

tax (ACT) which is equivalent to basic rate income tax and is recoverable by non-taxpayers.

The price of shares, and the income from them can fall as well as rise.

Advantages
Direct participation in future of company.

Disadvantages
Risk investment. Hidden charges.

Ideal use
Wealthier most sophisticated investors. Long term capital growth.

Taxation treatment
CGT on sales. Income tax deducted at source is recoverable. Tax reliefs on unquoted shares.

Chapter 20
Fixed Interest Stocks

Debentures
These are loans which are secured either on specific assets or by a floating charge over the assets of a company. They are the highest ranking company loan stock and any capital gains can now be exempt from tax. On a liquidation a debenture-holder gets preferential treatment. A well secured debenture with a company of good standing will usually yield more than a comparable gilt.

Preference shares
Like loan stocks preference shares are fixed interest. However, they are not loans but share capital. They rank ahead of ordinary shares on liquidation. Payment of preference dividends is made net of advance corporation tax (ACT) and the rate of return is usually, but not always, indicated in the title, eg 6% preference shares. There are a number of different types of preference shares, including;

- Cumulative, ie if a dividend is passed one year it will be paid later when profits allow.
- Participating, ie participating in profits over and above a certain level.
- Redeemable, ie the stock has a finite life and may sometimes offer a bonus on redemption.

Convertibles
A convertible is a fixed-interest stock, issued by a company, which carries the right to convert into ordinary shares of that same company at some future date. Most convertibles are based on unsecured loan stocks, but preference issues have been popular from time to time. The yield is likely to be lower than for a straight fixed interest issue and the stock will normally have a redemption date. The date or dates for conversion are pitched somewhat earlier than the redemption date. A convertible loan stock may have tax attractions to the issuing company and may be used in advance of a takeover, bid.

See also
- Bulldog Bonds
- Gilts
- Guaranteed Bonds
- Local Authority Investments

Advantages

Can offer a higher yield than gilts. Conversion rights.

Disadvantages

Can be difficult to understand (jargon). More risky than gilts.

Ideal use

To produce higher immediate income. Possibilities to convert to equities.

Taxation treatment

No composite rate tax. Probably no CGT.

Chapter 21
Friendly Societies

Tax exempt friendly societies
Friendly societies offer certain types of insurance policies which can accumulate in value completely free of any liability to tax. A conventional ten year endowment or maximum investment plan will suffer tax at the rates applicable to insurance companies on both income and capital gains within the policy. The preferential tax treatment afforded to friendly societies has been exploited and a number of new societies have been formed. This has led to a restriction on the amount which may be invested to £100 pa.

A policy with a friendly society may be attractive to the small saver but the charges within the plan should be examined to ensure they are not excessive. Also, if it is likely that the plan will be surrendered early there are penalties and in most cases the return is limited to the amount of premiums paid. These plans may be attractive if the underlying investment is a building society account.

Advantages
Simple administration. Disciplined savings.

Disadvantages
Restrictions on investment. Charges. Surrender penalties.

Ideal use
Small saver linking to a building society account.

Taxation treatment
Tax-free growth.

Chapter 22
Gilts

Conventional

Gilts are stock issued by the UK Government. A conventional gilt edged stock will either have a redemption date, eg 3% Treasury Stock 1990 or be undated, eg 3½% War Loan. Gilts can be purchased through the National Savings Stock Register or through a stockbroker. Where they are purchased through the Register, there is a limit to dealing of £10,000 per stock per day, and not all gilts are available. Interest is paid gross without deduction of tax at source (on Register gilts), although it is fully taxable.

Taxation

Capital gains from the disposal of gilts held for less than 12 months were chargeable to CGT if the disposal was made before 2 July 1986. The change in the tax treatment has been made in the light of the introduction of the measures to counteract the practice known as 'bond washing'. The new arrangements, called the 'accrued income scheme', apply to gilts and corporate bonds from 28 February 1986 and treat interest on stocks as accruing on a day to day basis between interest payment dates. Thus, on a sale the vendor will be charged to income tax on the income from the previous payment date to the date of sale and the purchaser will be charged to income tax on the income from the date of purchase to the date of the next payment date. The rules on bond washing are complex and professional advice should be sought where appropriate.

Low coupon short dated gilts offer extensive opportunities if you are a higher rate tax payer to obtain improved rates of return. This is because the gilts are purchased at a discount and part of the overall profit in holding the stocks to redemption comes in the form of a tax free capital gain.

Index-linked gilts

Redemption dates vary from 1988 to 2020. If you purchase £100 nominal of stock, you will receive a coupon income of 2% or 2% per annum, depending on the stock, paid half yearly. These payments are adjusted in line with changes in the RPI. The redemption value is likewise increased in line with the RPI. A sale prior to the redemption date will be at market price and may not reflect inflation over the period the stock has been held.

Advantages
Government backing. Wide choice of stocks. Marketability. Prices quoted in the press. Cash available from sale within 48 hours. Guarantees income for future years.

Disadvantages
Strict tax regime. Market forces.

Ideal use
Securing a fixed income. Inflation proof investment (index-linked).

Taxation treatment
Basic rate normally deducted at source but is recoverable, where appropriate. Exempt from CGT (after 2 July 1986). New 'bond-washing' rules.

Chapter 23

Guaranteed Bonds

How they work
These are insurance company bonds and the taxation treatment is usually the same as for single premium investment bonds. They offer a guaranteed rate of return fixed for the period that the life office specifies, eg 7% per annum for five years. The return can be taken in the form of income or as a lump sum at the end of the term, if a growth option is offered. The rates are subject to change based on market rates of interest.

The income is usually treated as paid after deduction of tax at the basic rate although it is not normally necessary to gross up. This could mean that guaranteed bonds are a more appropriate investment if you are over 65 and entitled to age allowance. It is not usually possible to recover the tax which is deemed to have been deducted at source.

Advantages
Guaranteed rate of return.

Disadvantages
Possible liability to tax at the higher rates.

Ideal use
Securing a fixed income. Over 65 and entitled to age allowance.

Taxation treatment
Usually no liability to basic rate tax. Usually no grossing up.

Chapter 24
Home Income Plans

Application

If you are over the age of 65 and require an income, you may be able to unlock some of the capital value tied up in your home to provide it. The Inland Revenue allows tax relief on the interest on a mortgage of up to £30,000 if at least 90% of the loan is used to purchase an annuity. The annuity is used to pay the interest on the mortgage, and some lenders will guarantee to hold the interest rate, with capital repayment on death.

> *Example:*
> *A male aged 75 pays tax at 30%, borrows £30,000 and applies 100% of the loan to purchase an annuity.*
>
> | *Annuity:* | *£ pa* |
> |---|---:|
> | *Capital element received* | *3,507* |
> | *Income element received (net)* | *1,353* |
> | *Mortgage interest paid (net)* | *(2,343)* |
> | *Net increase in spendable income* | *2,517* |

Repayment

If a home income plan is effected, the capital of the loan is normally repaid from the sale proceeds of the house following death. If death occurs shortly after the plan is effected then the estate will be reduced by the amount borrowed unless the annuity is guaranteed for any period or life cover is effected to protect the estate.

Inheritance tax planning

If extra spendable income is not required, it could be used to fund a life assurance policy under trust to save IHT.

Advantages

Unlocks capital value of own home to provide an income or for IHT planning.

Disadvantages
Reduction in estate. Fixed annuity but perhaps fluctuating mortgage interest.

Ideal use
For the elderly with insufficient income.

Taxation treatment
Tax relief interest on mortgages up to £30,000. Tax-free element of annuity.

Chapter 25
Inheritance Trusts

Introduction
This investment was designed to mitigate CTT, and had to be approached with caution.

Form
Inheritance trusts were not a special type of trust but a term coined by life assurance companies. In its original form it involved an interest free loan from the settlor to the trustees of a trust he had created for the purpose of making an investment in a single premium investment bond. The life assurance company provided the package of documentation and the advantage of using a bond was the ability to take a tax deferred income which in turn could be used to repay the loan.

As with discounted gift plans, the 1986 Finance Act's 'gifts with reservation' provisions have led to the removal of these schemes from the market. However, it is anticipated that some life assurance companies will introduce revised schemes. It will be essential to take professional advice on such schemes.

Chapter 26
Investment Bonds

Introduction
Single premium investment bonds are non–qualifying life assurance contracts where a lump sum investment is made. Tax liabilities are deferred and income can be capitalised at relatively low rates of tax. An 'income' can be taken each year free of any immediate liability to tax.

Funds
The capital, after deducting a front end charge (usually 5%), is invested in units in any of the funds operated by the life office. These funds generally cover most geographical areas (Japan, USA etc) and investment sectors (properties, equities etc). Some life offices offer 20 or more fund links including such specialist funds as a commodity fund and a technology fund. There is also a mixed or managed fund available where investments are made in other funds of the life office. It is usually possible to switch from fund to fund without triggering a tax charge and at nominal cost.

Taxation
Income is automatically accumulated within the life funds and suffers tax at the rate applicable to life offices, currently 29% or 35%. If you pay tax at basic rate, then an investment bond may not be an appropriate investment. Unit trusts may be more tax-efficient. If you do not pay tax at all then consider the investment carefully.

A tax deferred income is one of the advantages of a single premium investment bond. A withdrawal of up to 5% pa of the initial investment (on a cumulative basis) may be made without any immediate liability to tax. This facility is available for 20 years, by which time the whole of the original investment will have been withdrawn. Withdrawals in excess of these limits will be charged to income tax in the year they are made. The charge is not to basic rate tax but to higher rate tax only. Furthermore, there is no grossing up as with building society or bank deposit interest.

On death or final encashment the overall profit is liable to higher rate tax. The liability can be reduced by a claim to top-slicing relief. This relief is valuable and professional advice should be sought on the detailed calculations, preferably before a bond is acquired.

Advantages
Spread of investments. Simple paperwork. Tax-free switching.

Disadvantages
Complex tax rules. Charges.

Ideal use
Investors requiring tax-deferred income.

Taxation treatment
5% withdrawals tax-free. Top slicing relief. Higher rate charges (not basic rate).

Chapter 27

Investment Trusts

Introduction
Investment trusts are similar to unit trusts in their aims but they are structured very differently as they are formed as companies. Investment is made by purchasing shares which themselves are quoted on the Stock Exchange. A unit in a unit trust will be valued by the fund managers strictly by reference to the underlying assets of the fund. Investment trust shares are subject to market forces and generally trade at a discount to their net asset value. Some investment trusts are extremely large and the sector as a whole represents a sizeable proportion of the Stock Exchange all share index.

Compare with unit trusts
Investment trusts are not allowed to advertise, unlike unit trusts, and this may account for their low profile. They offer a similar spread of investments but a number of important points should be borne in mind. They can offer different types of capital including debentures, preference shares and convertible loan stocks. They can also offer warrants, which are not investments in the trust but a right to buy shares at a later date, at a price fixed when the warrants are issued. As with unit trusts, investment trusts do not pay capital gains tax.

The discount on investment trust shares may enable you to derive a greater income on your investment. If the discount is 20%, then for £1,000 invested you may derive an income from £1,250 worth of assets. However the same, or an even wider, discount may apply to a sale. Investment trusts have performed well over the longer term.

Split capital trusts
Some investment trusts have two different classes of capital and are known as 'split capital' trusts. They have a limited life and the ordinary share capital is divided into income shares and capital shares. The income shareholders receive each year the net income of the trust. On liquidation they receive only a fixed redemption value, usually the nominal value of the shares. Capital shareholders receive

no income but on liquidation receive all the capital appreciation on the trust's investments. There are variations on this basic theme.

Advantages
Discount to net asset values. Split capital trsust.

Disadvantages
Discount to net asset values. Lack of advertising.

Ideal use
Long–term equity investment. Investment abroad.

Taxation treatment
CGT deferral. Income tax on all income.

Chapter 28

Life Assurance

Introduction
The traditional role of life assurance has been to provide protection for your family and dependants and increasingly to meet future liabilities, eg school fees and mortgage repayment. In recent years, new life companies have introduced new products which have made saving or investing through life assurance policies extremely popular.

With profits v unit-linked
The new, younger life offices have captured a large share of the market for regular savings and investment. They have succeeded through aggressive marketing and by offering investment (unit) linked contracts. Many traditional offices now also have a unit linked subsidiary, or are offering unit linked plans.

With profits policies usually involve some form of minimum guaranteed benefits. At regular intervals, usually each year, reversionary bonuses are added to increase the guaranteed benefits. Once added, these bonuses cannot be taken away. Reversionary bonuses are allocated on a cautious basis and are intended to smooth out investment fluctuations. Some companies pay additional special bonuses to reflect good investment performance but these are not regular. At the end of the policy term most life offices pay a terminal bonus to supplement bonuses already added. Terminal bonuses are not guaranteed but they are an important element in the overall return. Some companies pay very large terminal bonuses (often over 50% of the total profit) and it may be worth noting the practice of the life office before investing. Both reversionary and terminal bonuses are currently at an all time high and may have to be reduced in the future unless very high investment returns can continue to be achieved.

A unit linked contract requires that each premium is allocated to units in a fund, either an authorised unit trust or an in-house life fund. The performance of the funds can be followed daily in the financial press and it is possible to switch from one fund to another. If you decide to invest in a unit linked contract, you should watch for 'capital' or 'initial' units under which heavy annual charges are made. 'Accumulation' units do not usually suffer such high charges. You should also watch for poor investment allocation as some companies restrict the amount of your premium actually allocated to buy units.

The best unit linked contracts have performed better than the best with profits policies. However, it is also true that the worst of the unit linked contracts have been much worse than the lowest with profits policies.

Life assurance premium relief (LAPR)

LAPR was abolished for new policies taken out after 13 March 1984. For policies which satisfy the qualifying conditions, and which were taken out before 13 March 1984, tax relief at 15% is due on the regular premiums provided they do not exceed the greater of:

- £1,500 pa gross and
- one sixth of your total income after deducting charges.

These limits are shared between a man and his wife.

If you are paying premiums under a policy effected before 13 March 1984, you are enjoying a valuable Inland Revenue subsidy. Care should be exercised when dealing with the policy, particularly in relation to options and to variations of the original contract, to ensure LAPR is not jeopardised. Such contracts should be surrendered as a last resort and professional advice should be sought before taking action.

It is also wise to consider the possibilities open to you in connection with a qualifying policy that is about to mature. Allowing the policy to mature may well be the last thing you should do – see below.

Trusts for life policies

Life assurance plans may be written upon trust or assigned to trustees in order to ensure that any growth accrues outside your estate rather than inside where it will merely aggravate the IHT position. If it is a regular premium plan, each premium will be treated as a gift although it is likely that each gift will fall within one or other of the lifetime IHT exemptions available each year.

The type of trust, the beneficiaries of the trust, and who should be trustees will depend on your own personal circumstances. However, flexible family trusts can be created under which the exact beneficiaries and their respective shares need not be determined at the outset. The inheritance tax rules concerning gifts with reservation will apply if you wish to be included amongst the beneficiaries.

113

Maturing life policies

If you have a life policy (endowment or maximum investment plan) which is about to mature then you should consider carefully whether to take the proceeds or leave the funds with the life office. There may be considerable advantages in continuing the policy, for example it may be possible to leave it to accumulate in value or to draw an income from it, in either event completely free of any personal tax liability. Care needs to be exercised if the policy has been made paid-up, if there are any loans outstanding, and particularly if the policy is held in trust.

Auctioned policies

If you are considering surrendering a life policy, you should also think about selling it to an investor who may well offer you more than the surrender value. There is an established market in with-profits policies.

From the investor's point of view, a purchased policy can offer a very attractive rate of return which will be subject only to capital gains tax.

Products

See also

- Capital Conversion Plans
- Friendly Societies
- Guaranteed Bonds
- Home Income Plans
- Investment Bonds
- Maximum Investment Plans

Chapter 29
Local Authority Investments

Yearlings
Many investors are aware of the benefits of investing in gilt edged stock, but it is not so often recognised that higher gross returns can be obtained from local authority or public sector stocks. These are similar to gilts (although there is no Government guarantee) and capital gains can now be exempt from tax. With the possibility of tax free capital gains the attractions of these stocks are real but suitable stocks are less freely available. The security is not as strong and competent professional advice is necessary.

Town Hall Bonds
Fixed term, fixed rate investments. The composite rate scheme of tax deduction applies.

See also
- Bulldog Bonds
- Gilts

Advantages
High gross return

Disadvantages
Not so freely marketable as gilts. Not as secure as gilts.

Ideal use
Securing high fixed income for fixed period.

Taxation treatment
Interest taxable and paid net. Capital gains can be tax free.

Chapter 30

Maximum Investment Plans

Introduction
An MIP provides a very attractive and straightforward way of establishing a tax sheltered investment fund in the UK. They are particularly attractive to higher rate taxpayers and there is no limit on the amount which can be invested.

The plan must conform to certain strict Inland Revenue requirements if it is to qualify. One of the most important of these is that ten annual contributions must be made. These premiums may be met out of income or by committing a lump sum of capital. The plan is most commonly investment linked but there are with profits versions available.

Example
There is very little life cover in an MIP as the maximum amount of each premium is allocated to investment. As an example of the potential of an MIP, a premium of £1,000 pa might accumulate a fund of £17,000 after 10 years. The profit of £7,000 is free of personal tax liability. The options available to the policyholder may include:

- leave the £17,000 with the life office to grow free of personal tax liability;
- leave the £17,000 with the life office and enjoy a *tax-free* income;
- extend the policy term and continue to pay premiums.

If the policy is written as a cluster of small policies, it may be possible to exercise all three options simultaneously. To obtain an IHT advantage the policies may be arranged under trust.

Advantages
Professional investment management. Simplified administration.

Disadvantages
Hidden costs. Early surrender penalties. Sometimes inflexible during first ten years.

Ideal use
Higher rate taxpayers. Planning for retirement.

Taxation treatment
Maturity proceeds free of income tax and CGT and possibly IHT.

Chapter 31

National Savings

Some of the National Savings products are exceptionally competitive particularly for higher rate taxpayers. It is also possible for trusts to hold National Savings Certificates, including the yearly plan, and in certain circumstances it is possible to transfer certificates to trustees. The maximum holdings of National Savings products apply to a husband and wife separately.

NSB Ordinary Account
Pays interest at 6% pa for each calendar month in which the balance is at least £500, but you do not need to maintain that balance all year round. You do need to maintain a balance of at least £100 all year. The first £70 of interest is tax free and the optimum balance is therefore £1,166.

NSB Investment Account
Offers a competitive rate of interest, currently 10.75% pa, which is paid gross but is fully taxable. One month's notice of withdrawal is required and interest accrues on a day-to-day basis. The investment account is outside the scope of the composite rate tax scheme which applies to almost all other banks. The maximum investment is £100,000.

National Savings Income Bond
Minimum investment £2,000, maximum £100,000. Interest is currently 11.25% pa variable at six weeks notice, paid monthly and without deduction of tax at source. Repayment is made at three months' notice and withdrawals in the first year are penalised.

National Savings Deposit Bond
Minimum investment £100, maximum £100,000. Interest is currently 11.25% pa variable at six weeks' notice credited annually and without deduction of tax at source. Repayment is made at three months' notice and withdrawals in the first year are penalised.

National Savings Certificates – 31st issue
Return totally free of income tax and CGT. If held for the full five

year term the annual interest rate is equivalent to a yield of 7.85% pa. Minimum investment is £25, maximum £5,000.

National Savings 3rd Index-Linked Certificates

Maximum investment £5,000 excluding holdings of other issues. Return totally free of income tax and CGT, and linked to changes in the retail prices index (RPI). A supplement of 2.5% is added in the first year, 2.75% in the second year, 3.25% in the third year, 4% in the fourth year and 5.25% in the fifth year. These 'granny' bonds are now available to anyone.

National Savings Indexed Income Bond

Minimum investment £5,000, in multiples of £1,000, maximum £100,000. The interest rate for the monthly income for the first year is 8% pa. This rate is increased at the end of each year to match increases in the RPI. There is no increase in capital values and income is fully taxable although paid without deduction of tax at source.

National Savings Yearly Plan

The yearly plan is a regular savings scheme which replaces the old SAYE. Monthly payments are made between £20 and £200. At the end of 12 months a yearly plan savings certificate is purchased. If the certificate is held for a further four years the overall return, after five years, is 8.19% pa compound, tax free. The return is lower if the certificate is encashed early. Payments can continue after 12 months to purchase further certificates.

General extension rate

After the initial investment term has expired, National Savings Certificates may be left invested and will attract 'interest' at the general extension rate—currently 8.01% pa tax free. This is exceptionally attractive for higher rate taxpayers.

Advantages

Simple to understand. Purchased at Post Offices. No charges.

Disadvantages

Low maximum investments.

Ideal use

Low risk investment. Suitable for higher rate taxpayers.

Taxation treatment

No composite rate tax. Certificates free of income tax and CGT.

Chapter 32

Offshore Funds

Introduction
The wide variety of offshore funds act like unit trusts and invest on a global scale in stocks and shares. There are also 'roll-up' funds which in various ways convert highly taxed investment income into capital gains. The Finance Act 1984 ensured that these gains will now be taxed as income rather than capital gains. The new legislation will not apply to those funds which distribute all or most of their income. The rules are very complicated but you should ask at the outset whether a particular fund has or has not obtained 'distributor status'.

Tax deferral
It is amongst the funds which have not obtained distributor status that some interesting investment opportunities may be found. A managed currency fund trades in a spread of currencies across the world in order to maximise gains. There is no income tax liability until the investment is sold. This deferral is useful if you expect to be in a lower tax bracket, or not liable to income tax at all, in the future.

Umbrella funds
Amongst the offshore funds some management groups offer umbrella funds. Strictly, these are not unitised funds; instead you purchase redeemable participating preference shares which are quoted on the Stock Exchange. Switching can be arranged free of capital gains tax and usually there are both equity and currency funds under the umbrella. There is often quite a high minimum investment required and the suitability of a particular arrangement should be considered carefully.

Advantages
Wide range of funds.

Disadvantages
Complex tax rules. Lack of regulation. Charges.

Ideal use
Expatriates. Individuals not domiciled in the UK.

Taxation treatment
Possible CGT deferral. Possible income tax deferral.

Chapter 33

Personal Equity Plans

Introduction
The 1986 Finance Act includes provisions establishing a new scheme to commence on 1 January 1987. It is designed to encourage savings by individuals through the purchase of shares via a 'Personal Equity Plan' (PEP).

Maximum investment
The Finance Act provisions allow for detailed regulations to be made by statutory instrument, but the basic idea is that you will be able to invest up to £2,400 each year into your PEP. The proceeds from selling the shares comprised in the PEP, and the dividends received, may be retained in the PEP and used to purchase further shares, even if this takes you over the £2,400 ceiling.

Taxation
Any capital gains and reinvested dividends in the PEP will be entirely free of tax provided the investment in the PEP has been maintained for a complete calendar year. For example, if you invest at any time during 1987, the plan must be kept in force during 1988 but could be encashed tax free any time after 1 January 1989.

The plan will be operated by a plan manager who will reclaim the tax deducted on dividends on your behalf, but it is envisaged that the underlying shares will actually belong to you and will be registered in your name so that you can vote at meetings and will receive annual reports, etc.

At the time of writing details of the plan are still being considered by the Government and prospective plan managers.

Chapter 34

Property to Let

Property has traditionally been a good hedge against inflation. You benefit from the potential to increase income by regular rent reviews and from the capital growth in the rising value of the property. Generally speaking the purchase of property to let does not involve any tax allowances for the expenditure. However, capital allowances on 100% of the cost of an industrial or commercial building (ignoring any land content) are still available if the property is situated in an Enterprise Zone (see Chapter 18).

Furnished holiday letting
The income from let property is chargeable to tax after deducting certain expenses and, in the case of furnished lettings, a sum for depreciation of the furniture. An allowance may be claimed against the income from the property for interest paid on a loan to purchase or improve it. If the letting of property constitutes a business of providing 'furnished holiday lettings', the profits will qualify for special tax treatment. They are regarded as earned income and you can deduct from them an allowance for any pension premium you pay. Furthermore, any losses you make are allowable against your general income. You are entitled to both roll-over and retirement relief from capital gains tax.

Letting your home
If you decide to let part or all of your own home, when you sell it, part of your gain may be subject to CGT. However, there is a valuable relief available which can reduce the amount chargeable to tax by as much as £20,000. This relief is available in situations where you may not expect it: for example, when you decide to buy a second property and you elect for this to be treated as your main residence for CGT. If you keep your old property and let it as residential accommodation (not necessarily on a commercial basis), then subsequently sell it, the gain can be reduced for the length of time you lived in the property and by a further £20,000 for the period it was let.

Advantages
No limit on borrowing.

Disadvantages
Running costs and administration. Land law.

Ideal use
Low risk investment. Hedge against inflation.

Taxation treatment
Relief on borrowing. Possible capital allowances. CGT reliefs.

Chapter 35

Property to Live In

Your own home

The single largest investment that most people make in their lifetimes is the purchase of their own homes. Successive governments have encouraged home ownership by granting relief for loans to purchase or improve property used as the only or main residence of the borrower. The profit on the disposal of your only or main residence is exempt from capital gains tax.

Many people have to borrow to buy their homes but, even if you have sufficient capital resources, a loan which qualifies for tax relief is often a sound proposition. Such a loan will free capital for investment elsewhere and the income that this generates could be used to service the borrowing.

The interest on the first £30,000 of loans to purchase or improve your own home qualifies for tax relief. Borrowing money, even to purchase property, which does not qualify for tax relief is expensive. Tax relief for loan interest is granted at source under MIRAS (mortgage interest relief at source) and even non-taxpayers can qualify.

Mortgages

Because of the way most building societies operate MIRAS, it can be cheaper to repay a mortgage by means of a low cost endowment policy or a pension policy rather than a conventional repayment mortgage. Many lenders average out the interest and capital owing so that net repayments remain constant unless interest rates or tax rates change.

Under the low cost endowment or pension method of financing a mortgage no capital is repaid until the end of the mortgage term. You pay interest, sometimes at a rate above the rate charged on a conventional mortgage. The capital is repaid out of the proceeds when the low cost endowment matures – these arise tax free – or from the tax free cash available when you commute part of your pension. When calculating the premiums for either the low cost endowment or the pension policy the lending organisation will need to have regard to the future bonuses which may be added. Most lenders will take account of 80% of illustrated reversionary bonuses and will ignore the terminal bonuses.

Organisations do not have the same criteria when assessing low cost endowment and pension policies for lending purposes. Some do not charge a premium over the rate for conventional mortgages. Some take account of 100% of reversionary bonuses. The premiums can be reduced significantly depending on the position of the lender. Furthermore, the projections of some life companies, estimating present or future bonuses, can be significantly better than others. It is wise to shop around and to seek professional advice, in view of the sums involved and the long term nature of the commitment.

This table illustrates the cost and possible benefits of the three methods of funding a mortgage.

A male aged 40 next birthday pays tax at basic rate and wishes to borrow £30,000.

	Building Society repayment mortgage	Low-Cost Endowment mortgage from bank	Pension mortgage
Interest rate (gross)	11%	11%	11%
Mortgage repayment (net)	£230.41	£195.25	£195.25
Mortgage protection policy	7.60	–	5.61
Low cost endowment premium	–	43.30	–
Pension premium (net)	–	–	41.22
Monthly cost	£238.01	£238.55	£242.08
Cash surplus after mortgage repaid	–	£21,047	£24,030
Pension for life	–	–	£16,182 pa

If you decide on a pension policy of the type available to the self-employed or those in non-pensionable employment, this will only be available so long as you remain as such. If you cease to be self-employed and become a member of a company pension scheme, apart from where the scheme provides death benefits only, then you will no longer qualify for this type of policy.

Advantages
Low risk investment. Repayment methods. Mortgage frees capital.

Disadvantages
Running costs. £30,000 effective limit on mortgages. Insurance protection required.

Ideal use
Ability to purchase a more expensive property.

Taxation treatment
Tax relief on mortgages. No CGT on increase in value.

Chapter 36

Property to Share

Timesharing

Timesharing involves the purchase of a week, or unit, in a holiday development for use year after year. It is a relatively popular and inexpensive way to acquire a second property. However, a potential purchaser should tread warily as there have been a number of business failures and sales of timeshare properties where inadequate market research was made. Look at the service charges and the possibilities of re-sale. There can also be complex legal problems, particularly with overseas properties.

There are possibilities to exchange weeks and there are specialist exchange organisations to cater for this. Whether a timeshare will prove a good long term investment will depend on the quality of the development and how it becomes established.

There is some consumer protection offered by the British Property Timeshare Association and it is possible to buy insurance which provides a 'fighting fund' if the management company handling the timeshare gets into difficulties.

The tax consequences for the disposal of a timeshare may depend on whether, when acquired, the timeshare was for a period which exceeded 50 years. If less than 50 years, the timeshare may be considered a 'wasting asset' for CGT purposes and as such there will be a restriction on the extent to which the acquisition price is deductible from the sales proceeds. There are also difficulties in obtaining any tax relief for interest on a loan to purchase a timeshare.

Advantages
Lower cash outlay than buying second property or holiday home.

Disadvantages
Costs. Longer term 'investment'. Restrictions on exchange. Possible legal problems.

Ideal use
Possibly for a company to provide 'perks' to employees.

Taxation treatment
If a 'wasting asset' then CGT complications.

Chapter 37

Traded Options

Introduction

A traded option gives the right to buy or sell a particular share at a pre-established price over a given period. An option to buy a share is known as a 'call' option, and one giving the right to sell a share is known as a 'put' option. Unlike a conventional option a traded option can be bought and sold almost as if it were a share itself. Prices of traded options are quoted on the Stock Exchange. There are over 70 major quoted companies in whose shares you can trade options.

> *Example: You expect the price of World Chemicals shares to rise from their current price of £2.54 to £3.00. An option to buy World Chemicals shares for £2.60 each at any time in the next four weeks costs 15p.*
>
> *If World Chemicals shares rise to £3.00 and you had bought the option for 15p you would have made 25p per share. That is the difference between the market price of £3.00 and the option price of £2.60 less the cost of the option. Instead of exercising the option the traded options market allows the option itself to be sold and it is likely that the market will pay at least 40p for the option.*
>
> *Although the share price of World Chemicals has risen by just over 18% you have made over 166%, by purchasing the option. If the price does not rise, you do not exercise your option and you lose 15p per share.*

It is essential to seek professional advice before entering the traded options market as the structure of a traded options contract is complex. Profits arising from traded options are usually subject to CGT.

Advantages
Potential to boost profits from share price movements.

Disadvantages
Complex investment medium.

Ideal use
Hedging a rise or fall in the price of a stock.

Taxation treatment
Usually CGT.

Chapter 38
Unit Trusts

Introduction
There are now over 800 unit trusts on offer, some from very large management groups. The trusts themselves invest their funds in a wide variety of ways. There are trusts investing in oil exploration, health care, and penny shares in addition to the more general UK equity trusts. The choice of which trust to invest in will depend on your attitude to risk, your requirement for income and your view of the future, amongst other things.

Costs
Unit trusts can be purchased and sold with relative ease and the charges are fairly standard, being 5% initially and ¾% pa. Many fund managers and others offer a management service if you have a larger sum to invest. For a fee the managers will invest in a range of unit trusts and provide both valuations and advice on switching. The service is often cheaper where you give the managers discretion to switch as and when they decide, without prior consultation with you.

Managed funds
A new product which has recently become available is the managed fund or 'fund of funds'. The basic idea is that the unit trust invests in units of other trusts managed by the same company. The charges are strictly controlled in view of the fact that this particular arrangement has been exploited in the past and investors have lost money.

Overseas investment
Following the suspension of exchange controls unit trusts have invested considerable sums abroad. The use of unit trusts based in the UK may circumvent some of the practical and taxation problems inherent in investment abroad (eg investment advice, withholding taxes, etc). Alternatively, many reputable groups operate international unit trusts based outside the UK but investment in these funds should be considered carefully as there may be tax problems.

Advantages
Minimal paperwork. Spread of investment. Professional investment. Income can be reinvested.

Disadvantages
Bewildering array of funds. Tax charges for switching.

Ideal use
Long-term equity investment. Investments abroad.

Taxation treatment
CGT deferral. Income tax on all income.

Chapter 39
Woodlands

Introduction
An investment in woodlands may well produce substantial long term benefits. Larger sums are required but woodlands are assets which are likely to appreciate in real terms when measured against inflation. There are both grants and tax concessions to encourage forestry development.

Taxation
Some of the tax considerations relating to woodlands are:

Income tax:
The planting and maintenance costs of commercial woodlands can be set against the occupier's general income to create allowable losses. The interest paid on loans to acquire and develop woodlands is an allowable expense. Capital allowances (albeit reduced) are also available. When trees are to be felled a change of occupier may be arranged to ensure the favourable Schedule B basis of assessment applies. Under Schedule B there is a fixed assessment each year which normally amounts to no more than 50p per hectare pa.

Capital gains tax:
The value of standing timber and underwood is not chargeable to CGT. However, the land is chargeable. Roll-over relief is available following a sale.

Inheritance tax:
There are important reliefs from IHT. These include the treatment of commercially managed woodlands as business property (relief at 50%) or the deferral of IHT on growing timber until it is felled or sold.

Advantages
Can have other attractions (eg fishing). Grants.

Disadvantages
Cash flow. Sensitive to weather and pests.

Ideal use
Long term investment. Higher rate taxpayers.

Taxation treatment
Ideally Schedule D in early years and Schedule B later on. No CGT on standing timber.

Chapter 40

Zero–Coupon/Deep Discounted Bonds

Introduction
These are fixed interest securities which yield little or no income but a large capital gain at maturity. The capital gain may be liable to income tax and the Finance Act 1984 contains specific legislation to deal with the tax position of the issuing company and the individual investor.

Deferring tax
This type of investment can be very useful if you wish to defer investment income until a future year when your tax rate may be lower. Since the return is fixed it is possible to lock into a rate of return which is not subject to variations in interest rates.

An alternative investment along similar lines is the stripped US Treasury bond. These are commonly known as CATS (Certificates of Accrual on Treasury Securities) or TIGRS (Treasury Investment Growth Receipts). Due to the unfavourable tax rules stripped UK Gilts have not been marketed, although one issue of ZEBRAS (Zero-Coupon Eurosterling Bearer or Registered Accruing Securities) has been made but restricted to institutional investors.

Advantages
Income is rolled-up. Guaranteed rate of return.

Disadvantages
Complex tax rules. Restricted market.

Ideal use
Expatriates. Not for widows and orphans.

Taxation treatment
Possible income tax deferral.

Appendices

Appendix 1: Income Tax Checklist

1   What is my highest rate of tax in the current year?
2   What do I estimate my income to be over the next three years?
3   Do I have any scope for advancing or deferring income?
4   Am I sure about my residence status?
5   Am I sure about my domicile status?
6   (Non domiciled) Have I arranged my affairs so that I am only remitting capital?
7   Is it worth my while leaving the UK?
8   Have I claimed all the allowances to which I am entitled for the past 6 years?
9   Should I make any claim for loss relief?
10 Should I be considering a wife's earnings election?

Appendix 2: Capital Gains Tax Checklist

1   Am I sure about my residence and ordinary residence status?
2   (Non domiciled) Have I arranged my affairs so that I am remitting only non taxable capital?
3   Should I make disposals before 5 April to use the full relief for this tax year?
4   Should I defer disposals until 6 April so that I can delay paying the tax?
5   Am I making full use of my annual exemption?
6   Should I elect to have assets valued at 31 March 1982 for indexation purposes?
7   Should I elect to have a 6 April 1965 valuation?
8   Am I using losses to the best effect?
9   Are there advantages in claiming hold-over relief?
10   Is it worth my while leaving the UK?

Appendix 3: Inheritance Tax Checklist

1   What is the actual value of the loss to my estate as a result of the transfer I am proposing?
2   Am I sure about my domicile status?
3   Should I be considering using overseas entities to hold my UK assets?
4   Am I making full use of potentially exempt transfers?
5   Have I used all my nil rate band?
6   Is there scope for transfers to my spouse?
7   Am I taking full advantage of the annual exemption?
8   Can I use more of the other exemptions available?
9   Can I take advantage of holding assets through a trust?
10 Do the assets I am considering transferring qualify for business property relief or agricultural property relief?

Appendix 4: Time Limit Checklist

By 5 April 1987

1 Any person within the scope of charge to income tax or capital gains tax must, unless income and gains have been reported, give notice that he is so chargeable within one year after the end of that year.

2 An election or the revocation of an election for the separate assessment of wife's earned income for 1985/86.

3 Farmers' elections for herd basis and/or the averaging of profits for 1984/85.

4 Claims for the relief of 1983/84 and/or 1984/85 trading losses against the general income of that year.

5 Unless other time limits are provided elsewhere, a claim must be made within six years of the end of the year of assessment to which it relates. Therefore 1980/81 claims must be made by 5 April 1987.

By 4 June 1987

Where an option to acquire shares has been exercised during 1986/87 an election to pay tax by instalments must be made by 4 June 1987.

By 6 July 1987

1 Elections by married persons for separate assessment for income tax purposes should be made within six months before 6 July in the year of assessment. Elections to be effective for 1987/88 must be made by 6 July 1987.

2 An election to relate back qualifying retirement annuity premiums paid in 1986/87 to 1985/86 or, if there was no relevant earnings for that year, back to 1984/85.

3 Lloyd's Underwriters (Working Names) may relate retirement annuity premiums paid in 1986/87 back to 1983/84 if relevant earnings are taxable for the earlier year.

This list is not exhaustive; if in doubt, seek professional advice.

Appendix 5: Tax Facts

Income tax rates

1986/87 Taxable Income £	Band £	Rate %	Tax on Band £	Cumulative Tax £
17,200	17,200	29	4,988	4,988
20,200	3,000	40	1,200	6,188
25,400	5,200	45	2,340	8,528
33,300	7,900	50	3,950	12,478
41,200	7,900	55	4,345	16,823
Remainder		60		
1985/86				
16,200	*16,200*	*30*	*4,860*	*4,860*
19,200	*3,000*	*40*	*1,200*	*6,060*
24,400	*5,200*	*45*	*2,340*	*8,400*
32,300	*7,900*	*50*	*3,950*	*12,350*
40,200	*7,900*	*55*	*4,345*	*16,695*
Remainder		*60*		

Income tax reliefs

	1985/86 £	1986/87 £
Single Personal and Wife's Earnings	2,205	2,335
Married Personal Allowance	3,455	3,655
Additional Personal Allowance	1,250	1,320
Age Relief–Single Person	2,690	2,850
–Married Couple	4,255	4,505
–Excess over personal allowance reduced by ⅔ of income over	8,800	9,400
Maximum loans for interest on main residence	30,000	30,000
Dependent Relatives		
Single woman claimant	145	145
Married man or woman claimant	100	100
Housekeeper	100	100
Blind Person	360	360
Daughter's or Son's Services	55	55
Widow's Bereavement Allowance	1,250	1,320

Retirement annuity payments

Year of Birth	% of Net Relevant Earnings	
	1985/86	1986/87
1934 and after	*17.5*	17.5
1916–33	*20.0*	20.0
1914–15	*21.0*	21.0
1912–13	*24.0*	24.0
1910–11	*26.5*	26.5
Life Assurance	*5.0*	5.0

Car scale benefits

Age of car on 5 April	*1985/86*		1986/87	
	Under 4 years	*4 years & over*	Under 4 years	4 years & over
Value	***Up to £17,500***		**Up to £19,250**	
Up to 1300cc	*£410*	*£275*	£450	£300
1301–1800cc	*£525*	*£350*	£575	£380
Over 1800cc	*£825*	*£550*	£900	£600
Value	***£17,501–£26,500***		**£19,251–£29,000**	
All cars	*£1,200*	*£800*	£1,320	£875
Value	***Over £26,500***		**over £29,000**	
All cars	*£1,900*	*£1,270*	£2,100	£1,400

150% Scale if business miles 2,500 or less and for second company cars.
50% Scale if business miles 18,000 or more.

Car fuel benefit

At same rates and in same bands as benefit scales for cars under 4 years in basic (cc) scale.

50% Scale if business mileage is 18,000 or more.

Capital gains tax

1985/86		1986/87	
Gains	*Rate*	**Gains**	**Rate**
Individuals	*%*	**Individuals**	**%**
First £5,900	*Nil*	First £6,300	Nil
Thereafter	*30*	Thereafter	30
Trusts		**Trusts**	
First £2,950	*Nil*	First £3,150	Nil
Thereafter	*30*	Thereafter	30

Inheritance tax

Transfers made on or after 18 March 1986

	LIFETIME			DEATH★	
Tax £	Rate %	Gross transfers £		Rate %	Tax £
0	0	0- 71,000		0	0
3,600	15	71,001- 95,000		30	7,200
9,550	17.5	95,001-129,000		35	19,100
16,550	20	129,001-164,000		40	33,100
26,000	22.5	164,001-206,000		45	52,000
38,750	25	206,001-257,000		50	77,500
55,250	27.5	257,001-317,000		55	110,500
	30	over 317,000		60	

Main Exemptions

Lifetime rate on gifts between individuals	Nil
Lifetime rate on gifts into accumulation and maintenance trusts	Nil
Annual gifts per donor	£3,000
Small gifts per donee	£250

★This rate will also apply to gifts made within seven years of death, subject to a tapering relief for gifts made between three and seven years before death.

National insurance contributions

1986/87
Class 1 Employee

From 6 April 1986

Total weekly earnings	Contracted In Employee	Employer	Contracted Out Employee	Employer
Up to £38.00	NIL	NIL	NIL	NIL
£38.00-£59.99	5%★	5%★	2.85%†	0.90%†
£60.00-£94.99	7%★	7%★	4.85%†	2.90%†
£95.00-£139.99	9%★	9%★	6.85%†	4.90%†
£140-£285	9%★	10.45%★	6.85%†	6.35%†
over £285	(Note 1)	10.45%★	(Note 2)	(Note 3)

★ on all earnings

† on earnings over £38.00. The first £38.00 is charged at the contracted in rate appropriate to the level of earnings.

Note 1 Employee's maximum contribution is 9% of £285 (ie £25.65).

Note 2 Employee's maximum contribution is 9% on first £38.00 plus 6.85% on earnings between £38.00 and £285 (ie £20.34).

Note 3 10.45% on first £38.00 plus 6.35% on earnings between £38.00 and £285 plus 10.45% on excess over £285.

Prior to 6 April 1986 the same rates applied but the earnings bands were fixed at £35.50, £55, £90, £130 and £265.

Class 2 Self Employed (earning over £2,075 pa)
from 6 April 1986 £3.75 pw

Class 3 Voluntary from 6 April 1986 £3.65 pw

Class 4 Self Employed
from 6 April 1986 6.3% on profits £4,450–£14,820

Social security benefits

(pw)	from 25.11.85 £	from 28.7.86 £
Basic Retirement Pension		
– Single Person	*38.30*	38.70★
– Married Couple	*61.30*	61.95★
Child Benefit	*7.00*	7.10
Unemployment – basic	*30.45*	30.80
– addition for spouse (subject to earnings)	*18.80*	19.00

★ Increases from 28.7.86 not taxable 1986/87

Index

Neville Russell Chartered Accountants   **Confidential**
Personal Financial Planning Questionnaire

1 Your Name

Name _____

Address _____

. _____

Home telephone _____

Office telephone _____

2 Your Objectives

Taxation		**Investment**		**Other**	
Reduce income tax	☐	Accumulate personal capital	☐	Children's education	☐
Reduce corporation tax	☐	Capital investment for:		Providing for retirement	☐
Plan tax-free income	☐	growth	☐	Providing security for family	☐
Mitigate CTT	☐	increased net income now	☐	_____	☐
Use CTT exemptions	☐	increased income in future	☐	_____	☐

3 Personal Details

Your full name_____

Occupation_____

Date of Birth_____   State of health_____

Full name of spouse_____

Occupation_____

Date of Birth_____   State of health_____

4 Family Details

Full names of children	Date of birth	Occupation	Tick if married	Ages of grandchildren
_____	_____	_____	_____	_____
_____	_____	_____	_____	_____
_____	_____	_____	_____	_____
_____	_____	_____	_____	_____
_____	_____	_____	_____	_____
_____	_____	_____	_____	_____

5 Income Summary

Gross income	Self	Spouse
Earned income (please show below details of any fluctuating amounts and benefits in kind)	£_____	£_____
Investment income (including trust income)	£_____	_____
TOTALS	£_____	£_____

6 Capital Summary

Please give approximate values	Self	Spouse	Gross income arising p.a.
Assets			
Principal residence (joint tenants/tenants in common?)	£_____	£_____	£_____
Contents, chattels, etc.	£_____	£_____	£_____
Agricultural land	£_____	£_____	£_____
Other real property	£_____	£_____	£_____
Quoted stocks and shares (including unit trusts (please attach portfolio valuations)	£_____	£_____	£_____
Private company shares	£_____	£_____	£_____
Business assets (including goodwill) as partner/sole trader	£_____	£_____	£_____
Lloyd's Funds (as overleaf)	£_____	£_____	£_____
Trust Funds (please attach full details)	£_____	£_____	£_____
Bank current account	£_____	£_____	£_____
Bank deposit account	£_____	£_____	£_____
Building Society account	£_____	£_____	£_____
National Savings	£_____	£_____	£_____
Other assets (please specify)	£_____	£_____	£_____
	£_____	£_____	£_____
TOTAL	£_____	£_____	£_____

Liabilities			**Interest payable**
Mortgage outstanding repayment/endowment repayment date:	£_____	£_____	£_____
Bank loans and overdrafts	£_____	£_____	£_____
Other liabilities (please specify)	£_____	£_____	£_____

7 Wills

Please send us a copy of your latest wills or summarise them below:

Self: **Spouse:**

Do your wills reflect your current intentions?   Yes/No

8 Gifts

Please detail gifts made in the last 10 years by you or your spouse

Date	Donor	Beneficiary Self/Spouse	Property given	Value

If a trust has ever been created please forward trust deed or detail on a separate sheet.

9 Lloyd's Names

	Self	Spouse	Income
Deposits *	£	£	£
Personal reserves	£	£	£
Special reserve fund	£	£	£

* If you utilise a bank guarantee or letter of credit,
please indicate the amount and state the collateral you have pledged.

10 Retirement

	Self	Spouse
Anticipated retirement age	£	£
What benefits are anticipated at retirement?	£	£
Personal pension plan/company pension scheme. Will these benefits be sufficient?	£	£
What benefits are anticipated on death before retirement?	£	£
What do you pay towards these?	£	£

11 Life Policies

For each policy list the following:

On whose life? _____ _____ _____

For whose benefit? _____ _____ _____

Type of policy
eg whole life
    endowment bond _____ _____ _____

Name of company _____ _____ _____

Sum assured _____ _____ _____

Present bonuses _____ _____ _____

Date of commencement _____ _____ _____

Policy term _____ _____ _____

Annual outlay _____ _____ _____

Please forward any other information you feel may be relevant.

12 General

Is your spendable income sufficient? _____

Please attach details, if:
    You or your spouse have any interest
    (current or future) in any trust fund? _____

    You anticipate any change in your capital
    position (by inheritance or otherwise) _____

How much income is saved on a regular basis
and by what medium? _____

Do you make any regular income payments,
eg: Deeds of Covenant, alimony, etc)? _____

Any further relevant information may be included in a covering note.

13

If you wish to become a new client, you may return this form to any
Neville Russell Office or to Andrew Burgess,
Neville Russell, 246 Bishopsgate, London EC2M 4PB

Date:

Neville Russell offices:

Bedford, Birmingham, Brighton, Bristol, Dudley, Glasgow, Guildford, Harrow, Ilford, Leeds, Lincoln, London, Luton, Manchester, Milton Keynes, Norwich, Oxford, Poole, Skegness, Stockport, Sutton, Wakefield